How to be a
MOGUL

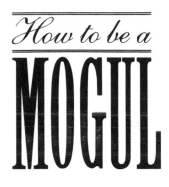

How to be a MOGUL

For those who know the best things in life are things

*By Diane Hartford,
Lynn Phillips, Milo Steale,
and Rusty Unger
Illustrations by Anthony Haden-Guest*

Clarkson N. Potter, Inc./Publishers
Distributed by Crown Publishers, Inc. New York

Copyright © 1986 by Diane Hartford, Ann
Scharffenberger, and Milo Steale
Illustrations copyright © 1986 by
Anthony Haden-Guest
Published by Clarkson N. Potter, Inc., 225
Park Avenue South, New York, New York
10003
CLARKSON N. POTTER, POTTER, and
colophon are trademarks of Clarkson N.
Potter, Inc.
Manufactured in the United States of America
Library of Congress Cataloging-in-Publication
Data
Main entry under title:
How to be a mogul.
1. Success—Anecdotes, facetiae, satire, etc.
I. Hartford, Diane.
PN6231.S83H67 1986   818'.5402
85-19120
ISBN 0-517-56019-4
10 9 8 7 6 5 4 3 2 1
First Edition
Lyrics from "Kansas City" reprinted with the
permission of Jerry Lieber.

Cheerfully designed by
Drenttel Doyle Partners

The
Mogul
Anthem

This land is my land

This globe is my globe

From Manhattan Island

To the papal earlobe

Da da da dum dum

Ta dum dum da da . . .

(Moguls are too busy
to complete anthems)

The authors wish to thank:

Kenneth Stanley Adams, Jr.,
Joseph Albertson,
Joe Lewis Albritton,
Albert Alkek,
Charles Allen, Jr.,
Herbert Allen,
Herbert Anthony Allen,
Robert Orville Anderson,
Walter Hubert Annenberg,
Philip F. Anschutz,
Edmund Newton Ansin,
Orvon Gene Autry,
Stewart Bainum, Sr.,
Edward Perry Bass,
Lee Marshall Bass,
Perry Richardson Bass,
Robert Muse Bass,
Sid Richardson Bass,
Frank Batten,
Carlton Beal,
Stephen Davison Bechtel, Sr.,
Stephen Davison Bechtel, Jr.,
Arthur Bejer Belfer,
Belk family,
Belz family,
Charles B. Benenson,
Arnold Bernhard,
Russel Berrie,
Morton K. Blaustein,
Paul Block, Jr.,
William Block,
Ivan Frederick Boesky,
Malcom Austin Borg,
Harvey R. Bright,
Edgar Miles Bronfman,
Jack Brown,
Warren Edward Buffett,
Dorothy Stimson Bullitt,
August Anheuser Busch, Jr.,
Cabot family,
Cargill/MacMillan family,
James R. Cargill,
Curtis Leroy Carlson,
Ben H. Carpenter,
Anne Cox Chambers,
Chandler family,
Harrison Gray Chandler,
James A. Clark,
Edward Baron Cohen,
Sherman Cohen,
Seymour Cohen,
Tristam C. Colket, Jr.,
Miles Collier,
Grover Connell,

Coors family,
Helen Kinney Copley,
Gardner Cowles family,
William Cowles family,
Edwin Lochridge Cox,
John Lee Cox,
William Coburn Cox, Jr.,
Henry Crown,
Lester Crown,

Acknowledgments

Cullen family,
Raymond L. Danner,
Joseph Morton Davidowitz,
Davis family,
Kenneth William Davis, Jr.,
Leonard Davis,
Marvin Davis,
Thomas Cullen Davis,
William Selden Davis,
Willametta Keck Day,
Edward John DeBartolo,
Robert H. Dedman,
John Cornelius Dempsey,
Dominique de Menil,
Clarence Douglas Dillon,
Richard Dinner,
Disney family,
Roy Edward Disney,
Nelson Doubleday, Jr.,
Sherman W. Dreisezun,
Louisa Copeland Duemling,
Alexis Felix du Pont, Jr.,
Helena Allaire du Pont,
Irénée du Pont, Jr.,
Pierre Samuel du Pont family,
Pierre Samuel du Pont III,
Willis Harrington du Pont,
Doris Duke,
David Durst,
Roy Durst,
Seymour Durst,
Charles Henry Dyson,
Alpheus Lee Ellis,
Jane Engelhard,
Entenmann family,
James Emmett Evans,
Thomas Mellon Evans,
Melanie Falk,
John Earl Fetzer,

William A. Fickling, Jr.,
Frederick Woodruff Field,
Marshall V. Field,
Firestone family,
Fisher family (Detroit),
Fisher family (Seattle),
Malcolm Stevenson Forbes,

Henry Ford II,
Josephine Clay Ford,
Kenneth W. Ford,
William Clay Ford,
Samuel Joseph Frankino,
Michel Fribourg,
Helen Clay Frick,
John Brooks Fuqua,
Daniel Mauck Galbreath,
John Wilmer Galbreath,
Francesco Galesi,
Ernest Gallo,
Julio Gallo,
Robert William Galvin,
Charles Cassius Gates,
Edward Lewis Gaylord,
Gordon Peter Getty,
Jean Paul Getty,
James Stanley Gilmore, Jr.,
Sol Goldman,
Katharine Graham,
Pincus Green,
Maurice Raymond Greenberg,
Margaretta Lammot du Pont Greenewalt,
Franklin Nelson Groves,
Robert Charles Joseph Edward Sabatini Guccione,
Amanda Guinzburg,
Gund family,
Haas family,
Evelyn Annenberg Hall,
Armand Hammer,
Floyd Roger Hardesty,
Harrah family,
William Averell Harriman,
Lita Annenberg Hazen,
David Whitmire Hearst,
George Randolph Hearst, Jr.,
Randolph Apperson Hearst,

William Randolph Hearst, Jr.,
Henry John Heinz II,
Harry Brakmann Helmsley,
Helen Hunt Hendrix,
Leon Hess,
Margaret Hunt Hill,
Henry Lea Hillman,
William Barron Hilton,
Oveta Culp Hobby,
Stanley Stub Hubbard,
Lamar Hunt,
Nelson Bunker Hunt,
Ray Lee Hunt,
Ruth June Hunt,
Ruth Ray Hunt,
Swanee Hunt (Meeks),
William Herbert Hunt,
Kyupin Philip Hwang,
James Leroy Jaeger,
Steven Paul Jobs,
Belton Kleberg Johnson
John Harold Johnson,
Jean Johnson,
Samuel Curtis Johnson,
Howard Brighton Keck
William Myron Keck II
Pauline MacMillan Keinath,
William Russell Kelly,
Kenan family,
Kennedy family,
Kirk Kerkorian,
John Werner Kluge,
James Landon Knight,
Philip Hampson Knight,
Charles de Ganahl Koch,
David Hamilton Koch,
Frederick Robinson Koch,
William Ingraham Koch
Joan Beverly Kroc,
Laird family,
Carl Clement Landegger
George Francis Landegger,
Estée Lauder,
Leonard Alan Lauder,
Ronald Steven Lauder,
Maurice Larry Lawrence
Norman Lear,
Samuel Jayson LeFrak,
Leon Levine,
Lilly family,
Carl Henry Lindner,
John Langeloth Loeb,
Daniel Keith Ludwig,
Jane Cox MacElree,
Alex Manoogian,
Armas Clifford Markkula, Jr.,

Introduction

HOW TO BE A MOGUL is a step-by-giant-step projection of your life as a Mogul, cradle to grave and beyond.

❧

As a Mogul, you do not have time to read introductions. As a Mogul, you only have time to tell your secretary to get this book for you so you can skim it (carefully) before giving it to another Mogul, which makes it a (deductible) business gift.

Marriott family,
John Franklin Mars,
Forrest Edward Mars, Sr.,
Forrest Edward Mars, Jr.,
Leonard Marx,
Mayer family,
McClatchy family,
McDonnell family,
Patrick Joseph McGovern,
McGraw family,
Malcom Purcell Mclean,
Gordon Barton McLendon,
Paul Mellon,
Richard Prosser Mellon,
Seward Prosser Mellon,
Timothy Mellon,
Bernard H. Mendik,
Sy Syms Merns,
August Christopher Meyer,
Gerrish Hill Milliken,
Minot King Milliken,
Roger Milliken,
William Alvin Moncrief, Jr.,
Moody family,
Gordon Earle Moore,
Robert Adam Mosbacher,
Mott family,
Clint William Murchison, Jr.,
David H. Murdock,
Rupert Murdoch,
Charles Haywood Murphy, Jr.,
Stephen Muss,
Donald Edward Newhouse,
Samuel Irving Newhouse, Jr.,
Arthur Charles Nielsen, Jr.,
Nordstrom family,
O'Connor family,
Yoko Ono,
Ordway family,
David Packard,
Max Palevsky,
William S. Paley,
Roy Hampton Park,
Jack Parker,
Allen E. Paulsen,
Luigino Francesco Paulucci,
Charles Shipman Payson,
Claude B. Pennington,
Henry Ross Perot,
Milton Petrie,

Pew family,
D. John Phillips,
Phipps family,
Howard Phipps, Jr.,
Generoso Paul Pope, Jr.,
Victor Posner,
Sol Price,
Abram Nicholas Pritzker,
Jay Arthur Pritzker,

Robert Alan Pritzker,
Pulitzer family,
The Ragliones,
Reed family,
Resnick family,
Donald Worthington Reynolds,
Marc Rich,
Robert Rich, Sr.,
Richardson family,
Meshulam Riklis,
Marshall Edison Rinker,
David Rockefeller,
Hope Aldrich Rockefeller,

John Davison Rockefeller IV,
Laurance Spelman Rockefeller,
Rodman Clark Rockefeller,
Chapman Root,
Henry A. Rosenberg, Jr.,
Ruth Blaustein

Rosenberg,
Rosenwald family,
Roush family,
Jack Rudin,
Lewis Rudin,
Richard Mellon Scaife,
Edith Schaffer,
Schnitzer family,
Caroline Hunt Schoellkopf,
E. W. Scripps family,
Edward Wyllis Scripps,
J. E. Scripps family,
Scully family,
Daniel Crow Searle,

William Louis Searle,
David B. Shakarian,
Shapiro family,
Bayard Sharp,
Hugh Rodney Sharp, Jr.,
Peter Sharp,
Robert Shelton,
Ann Phipps Sidamon-Eristoff,
Norton Winfred Simon,
Abby Rockefeller Simpson,
Leonard Samuel Skaggs,
Smith family,
Athalie Irvine Smith,
Frederick Wallace Smith,
Richard Alan Smith,
Vivian Leatherberry Smith,
Sheldon H. Solow,
James Sorenson,
Anne Windfohr Sowell,
Ray Stark,
Skip Stein,
Saul Phillip Steinberg,
Leonard Norman Stern,
Stone family,
George Strawbridge, Jr.,
Stroh family,
Sulzberger family,
Sydney Mark Taper,
Laszlo Nandor Tauber,
Louis Thalheimer,
Laurence Alan Tisch,
Preston Robert Tisch,
Donald John Trump,
Fred Charles Trump,
Robert Edward Turner III,
Sy Unger,
Upjohn family,
Jay Van Andel,
Robert Lee Vesco,
Lew R. Wasserman,
Sigfried Weis,
Leslie Herbert Wexner,
Whittenburg family,
Max Williams,
Wolfe family,
Wolfson family,
Robert Winship Woodruff,
William Bernard Ziff, Jr.,
Ezra Khedouri Zilkha,
William Zimmerman,
Mortimer Benjamin Zuckerman

. . . for providing us with inspiration for this book.

Alas! I am turning into a god!
—LAST WORDS OF EMPEROR VESPASIAN
(A.D. 79)

PART ONE

Going Mogul

The first trick in being a Mogul is to be able to know a Mogul when you see one. The second trick is to see one, because:

a. Moguls are short.
b. Their limo windows are tinted.
c. They don't fly coach.

1

By Their Lear Jets Ye Shall Know Them

All that glitters is not a Mogul. —JEREMOGUL 24:11

*M*oguls are people who crave money and power. As such, the Mogul Personality Profile superficially resembles nearly everyone else's.

Unlike many people obsessed with money and power, however, True Moguls:

1. Have money and power.
2. Want more.
3. Think they'd be happy if they were tall enough.
4. Are wrong about that. For a TRUE MOGUL, taller isn't enough; everything isn't enough; nothing is ever enough. Nothing.

SO DO NOT CONFUSE MOGULS WITH RICH PEOPLE.
Millionaires are a dime a dozen.
Moguls are not.

Rich people

Rich People	Moguls
Drive Cadillacs.	Are driven.
Fly the Concorde.	Own Lears.
Have yachts.	Have fleets.
Plant hedges.	Build compounds with electric fences.
Get candidates elected.	Decide who runs.
Go to the Symphony.	Build Lincoln Center.
Distrust the press.	Own the press.
Go to church.	Have private chapels.
Deduct all expenses.	Have Liberian citizenship.
Admire William F. Buckley.	Admire Attila the Hun.
Listen to Milton Friedman.	Never listen.
Give lavish dinner parties.	Throw galas.
Have alarm systems.	Hire bodyguards.
Ski St. Moritz.	Buy Alp.
Have country houses.	Have countries.
Go to Ivy League colleges.	Receive honorary degrees.
Strike oil.	Strike platinum.
Breed Lhasa Apsos.	Breed Polish Arabian horses.
Feel bad about Richard Nixon.	Feel bad about Robert Vesco.
Hate communists.	Hate governments.
Have secretaries with English accents.	Have children with English accents.
Take long vacations.	Take short naps.
Retire gracefully.	Become immortal.

AND DO NOT CONFUSE MOGULS WITH THE DALAI LAMA.
The Dalai Lama is a Meta-Mogul—
Mogul yet not Mogul.
True Moguls steer clear
of paradox.

← mogul

11

2

THE MOGUL'S WORLD
(Dun and Bradstreet Projection)

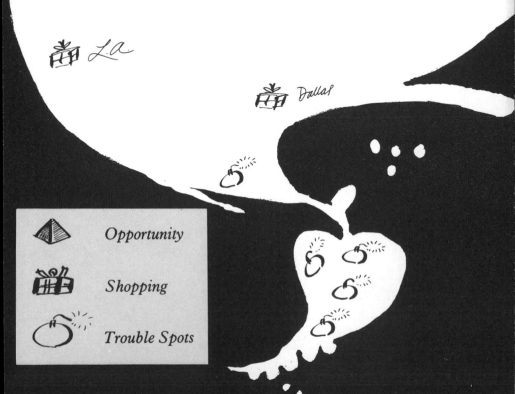

D.C.

L.A.

Dallas

	*Opportunity*
	Shopping
	Trouble Spots

3

THE MOGUL MOLD

*A Mogul by any other
name is still a Mogul.*

—WM. SHAKESMOGUL

*T*o be a Mogul you don't need family traditions, but you do need a knowledge of mogul tradition, as you will be expected to develop your mythic personality and signature style within certain recognizable parameters.

In the following tour of the Mogul Pantheon, find the archetype that best accommodates your abilities and aspirations. This is the model upon which your own mystique should be based.

1. Megalomogul

The progenitor of all Moguldom, the Megalomogul is descended directly from King Midas. The Megalomogul line was founded in the United States by John Jacob Astor, whose remark "More is better, and even more is even better" is pure Megalomogulese.

Well-known Megalomoguls: William Randolph Hearst, Ari Onassis, J. P. Getty, H. L. Hunt.

The Megalomogul's holdings include:
Big Horn Mountain
Big Muddy River (Big Bend
    National Park was donated to the
    government in 1967)
Big Sur (oil-drilling rights off coast of)

Favorite Personal Possessions: Big Ben, The Big Top Circus, Big guns

Favorite Theory: Big bang

Favorite Sports: Big Leagues, Big Ten

Favorite Business: Big Business

Favorite Occupation: The Big Board

Favorite Controversy: Big Foot

Favorite Star: Big Dipper

Favorite Cheese: Big Cheese

Favorite Bird: Big Bird

Favorite Pet: Secretariat

The Megalomogul's grandfather is famous for saying, when asked how much it cost him to buy Nottingsgateshire, England, for use as a boathouse, "If you have to ask, you're a damn fool!"

The Megalomogul's next of kin is . . .

2. The Great White Mogul, A.K.A.: Jaws

Nicknames: the Liquidator, the Prowler, the Raider.

Small for his size, but no anchovy, this wily fish preys on larger members of its own species, devouring Mogul empires, firing management, and dissolving company assets into hard currency.

Between meals, Jaws' cheeks appear deceptively flaccid, but while engaged in a "hostile takeover" his powerful mandibles fill with tough, folksy wit, swelling at times to such a great size he must conceal them behind banks of telephones and dummy corporations to prevent enemies from spotting him and devouring him first or to keep fans from mobbing him.

This newest and smallest species of Mogul is quickly proving to be its most colorful (wearing fewer white shirts than other Moguls) and the one with the highest impact on the economic ecosystem.

Examples of The Great White: Ted Turner, Carl Icahn, Saul Steinberg, T. Boone Pickens

As a Rule, Great Whites:

Do not keep appointment books.

Do not sing "Tomorrow" in the shower; do not sing "Yesterday" in the shower.

Did not set out to be sharks, just went with the flow.

Cannot be reached for comment.

Eat: lunch from a brown paper bag.

Threaten to eat: ITT, Big Oil, Big Media, any company sitting on real estate worth more than its product.

Favorite saying: "Show me a good loser, and I'll show you a loser."

Favorite story: David and Goliath

Favorite drug: Adrenalin

Favorite weapon: OPM (Other People's Money)

Biggest natural enemies: White Knights (corporations which rescue other corporations from his clutches by buying him out at an inflated price before he takes over and fires management); PAC Men (companies which try to acquire a controlling interest in Jaws' company before he can acquire a controlling interest in theirs)

Official parasites:

Arbitragers (pros who swim in the Great White's wake, investing in companies he's targeted for takeover in the hopes he'll drive the company's stock up)

Stockholders (amateurs whose stock tends to go up when a hungry Great White swims by)

Mates: Great Whites divorce women who understand them to marry women who understand finance. Unlike the usual Moguls, Great Whites consult their second wives on business.

3. Show-Biz Mogul ("Sho-Mo")

Has fun. Loves his work.

Loves his family.

Loves show business.

Tries to persuade offspring to choose another field.

Despite appearances, there are only three species of true Sho-Mos: HOLLYWOOD, BROADWAY, and RECORD. With the exception of Record Moguls, who unbutton all their top buttons and have mirrored desks, Sho-Mos are surprisingly sedate.

BROADWAY MOGULS are a dying breed. There are only two of them left, and they can't be kept in the same room long enough to mate.

HOLLYWOOD MOGUL

The typical Hollywood Mogul . . .
Wears: No socks
Registers: Democrat (even if he's Nixon's agent; votes for Reagan)
Owns: Own studio, talent agency, production company, or points
  in blockbusters
Also owns: Own parking space, pirated print of *E.T. II*, elaborate
  bathrooms, a Rembrandt etching
Favorite record: "Short People"
Favorite expression: "The American people do not understand
  irony."
Reads: Treatments, synopses; never scripts
Pretends to read: Books
Drugs: Producers use "on weekends"; agents give at the office.

NOTE: The popular image of a Hollywood Mogul is based on the activities of imitation or SHAM-MOGULS as much as on real ones. The four basic subspecies of Hollywood Sham-Moguls are:

MOGUL-IN-WAITING
(a.k.a. "Studio Head")

Because Studio Heads can be fired by New York–based CEOs of their studio's parent company, Studio Heads, often CALLED Moguls, can at best be Moguls-in-Waiting. The Mogul-in-Waiting can only become a full-fledged Mogul if his contract provides for over 2.3 mil in stock options and a six-picture production deal in a parachute clause when the MIW is fired for power grab or caught embezzling.

Most Notorious Mogul-in-Waiting: David Begelman
Least Notorious: Michael Eisner

ABBEY-RENTS MOGUL

Looks and lives exactly like a Hollywood Mogul, but his houses, cars, and clothes are all leased. His spending money is borrowed.

The Abbey-Rents Mogul always "has a project with Streisand" at Universal. Because this movie's never made, he never has a flop, and so can "live on borrowed time" indefinitely, depending on the quality of his press agent.

MOGULETTE

A woman of apparent power in Hollywood. No woman has real power in "the Industry," though a few are bankable.

Famous Mogulettes: Sue Mengers, Sherry Lansing, Barbra Streisand, Goldie Hawn, Esther Shapiro.

The only two differences in behavior between a Mogulette and Show Biz Mogul (Male) are:

Mogulettes usually choose first husbands from a more successful and older group than their own.

Mogulette's later husbands are hairdressers, fitness trainers, or
foreign filmmakers whom Mogulette remakes into producers
when she's ready to direct.

DEMI-MOGUL
(a.k.a. "Creative Genius")

While he CLAIMS to be motivated by powerlust and greed like
everyone else, the Demi-Mogul secretly sees himself as an Immortal Artist. As a result, although he has the money, power, and big-risk panache of a True Mogul, the Demi spends too much of his
time on artistic touches, pinball, Italian dinners, Italian gestures,
subtitles, mind alteration, and mood elevation for his own good.

Real Moguls BUY artists. Only Demi-Moguls try to BE them.

Prototype: Irving Thalberg
Best-known: Francis Ford Coppola

4. Moguline (Female Mogul)

Mogulines seem more frightening than other Moguls because they
remind you—however slightly—of your mother.
If you don't do what they tell you to do they might put you up for
adoption.

Every Moguline, living, dead, or in-between, has been described
in print at least once as having "an iron whim." Also, every Moguline:
Has breathed a sigh of relief that Truman Capote's manuscript of
Answered Prayers is still missing
Has her own personal shoulder-pad mold
Has a villa in Capri or Antibes
Has her house redecorated every twenty-eight days
Has a plastic surgeon who makes house calls on retainer
Has an alcoholic ex-husband
Has a handicapped younger sister
Has a son who never married
Has a daughter who attempted suicide and then wrote a book
about her
Has a banker either in her family or in her pocket.

Mogulines do not:
Sag, wrinkle, or bloat
Worry about having a date for New Year's Eve
Care about this really great sale at Benetton's
Know who Madonna is
Know where Toys 'R Us is
Know what double coupon days are
Know when you're only kidding

America's first Moguline was Hetty Green. Worth more than
$100 million when she died in 1916. Hetty, after inheriting her
father's fortune and swindling her ex-husband out of his, increased
her wealth ten times over by lending money to businessmen at

inflated interest rates. Her son's leg had to be amputated when she refused to pay doctors to treat him at New York's Bellevue Hospital where she had taken him, dressed in rags, as a charity case.

The truth is, Mogulines behave exactly the same as other Moguls except there are only three of them. Estée Lauder, Katharine Graham, and Yoko Ono are the only women on the "Forbes 400" list lately who run their own empires. Only Estée Lauder created hers from scratch.

Some experts feel women are too dumb to be Moguls, while some believe they're too smart to submit to the Mogul grind. Still others claim that Moguldom is a form of testosterone poisoning from which most women are immune.

5. Mogulanthropist

This Mogul, characterized by an addiction to established charities and uncontroversial causes, is known for his piety, his patriotism, his Upwardly Mogul wife, and his pink pants.

The Mogulanthropist aims:
To be on a Presidential Commission
to investigate waste in the
Department of Welfare
To be an ambassador
To own a President

The Mogulanthropist loves:
Publicity

The Mogulanthropist likes:
Five-course dinners in hotel
ballrooms
The Peter Duchin Orchestra
Visiting mistress before breakfast at
the Regency (N.Y.) or the
Beverly Hills Hotel (L.A.)
To believe his life is not boring

Favorite charities include:
Grosse Point Clean Air Association
Bhopal Fresh Air Fund
Metropolitan Museum of Art Fashion Wing
Philharmonic orchestras (New York and Palm Springs)
All stress diseases and cancers
The Republican Party

The Mogulanthropist is:
Donor: Burn Ward of New London Hospital (after son caught fire
free-basing at Groton)
Honorary Chairman: Dartmouth College Large-Type Library

A Mogulanthropist would never:
Deliberately cause his family pain.
Forget to take out flight insurance on family.
Spoil his son by giving him too much money.
Doom his daughter to marry a fortune hunter by giving her any money.

Mogulanthropist motto: *"Moglesse Oblige"*

6. Mystery Mogul

The source of the Mystery Mogul's wealth is always shrouded in doubt. No one has ever gone to school with him.

The Mystery Mogul has houses all over the world, but nobody knows where his office is.

The Mystery Mogul:
Wears: bulletproof Armani clothes (fitted on Rodeo Drive)
Pet peeve: questions.

Famous Mystery Moguls: Robert Vesco, Marc Rich, L. Ron Hubbard, Reverend Moon, Don Corleone

7. Global Mogul

The Global Mogul's heroes are Disraeli, Cromwell, Bismarck, and Metternich. A Global Mogul's biggest regrets are:
1. Having but one life to give for his country.
2. Not being king of that country.

While Megalomoguls don't travel abroad, a Global Mogul zooms around the world wielding influence in as many countries as possible. Often found behind the scenes, a Global Mogul has usually created the scenes in the first place.

Ailing corporations, bankrupt cities, wealthy widows, undeveloped countries, and destabilized governments all benefit from a Global Mogul's ministrations. The Power to Help not only enriches the Global Mogul, it makes him feel good inside. Also, it gets him invited to state funerals, where he is formally introduced to his next prospect. After all, kings come and go, but saviors get invited back.

The Global Mogul:

Gets Christmas presents from Princess Margaret, Castro, and Greta Garbo.

Was once married to Pamela Churchill Harriman.

Is the guest of honor at parties given by Lord Weidenfeld and Ann Getty.

Currently has a very tall wife who had a career before she married him.

Still gives Fabergé eggs to Lady Antonia Fraser at Easter.

Never gets jet lag.

Was the president's envoy to the Mideast.

Personally air-lifted Christmas dinners to POWs in 1967.

Has a book agent who is also a Mogul.

Once took Jacqueline Onassis to the opening of something.

FAMOUS GLOBAL MOGULS:

Walter Annenberg
Henry Ross Perot
Felix Rohatyn
Peter Grace
David Rockefeller

8. Upwardly Mogul

The Upwardly Mogul is hiding something other than the source of his wealth, i.e., his wealth.

(Arab and Italian Moguls living in the Galleria or any Trump building in New York, OR the Bel Air Hotel in Los Angeles may ALSO feel the need to conceal their wealth, but only in their own countries—where they never go.
Foreign Mogul pet fear: Kidnapping.)

Unlike other Moguls, the Upwardly Mogul worries that surface flash will distract from his superior human qualities.

The Upwardly Mogul:
Wears: Antique L. L. Bean, distressed cashmere
Turns down: Audience with Pope, or
Joins: Unitarian Church
Gives: to causes as opposed to charities
Buys: Summer house at Northeast Harbor, Maine
Dates: Gloria Steinem
Cuts: Buckles off Gucci shoes
Redesigns: The atrium, the toilet, *U.S. News and World Report*

FAMOUS UPWARDLY MOGULS:

Mort Zuckerman
Stuart Mott

9. Moguls in Progress

BABY MOGUL

Having made over thirty million while under thirty, the Baby Mogul has no style of his or her own, but doesn't know it, because is as yet unfamiliar with Mogul Tradition.

Habitat: Silicon Valley, Hollywood, the Brill Building in New York

Fixations: Oral, numerical (in millions)

Drugs: Helium

MINI-MOGUL

Has the most wealth and power in his town.

Example: Harold Hoffburger of the Hoffburger Sprocket Factory, Hoffburger, NH.

MICRO-MOGUL

Has the most wealth and power in his neighborhood.

Example: Dino Gatsbino, Sr., of Eat-Rite Pizza, S. Phila., PA.

10. Yoguls

Yoguls try but don't have what it takes to be a Mogul.

Yoguls:
Ask for coat checks at "21."
Sit at center tables in the Russian Tea Room.
Fly to Los Angeles without deducting trip.
Get caught passing insider tips to their secretaries and forget to plead *nolo contendere.*
Get caught taking their secretaries as "paid consultants" on Presidential Commission trips to Barbados.
Buy cocaine from cops on camera.
Put money in a Brazilian bank and ask Switzerland for asylum.

4

MOGUL YOUTH

God bless the child who makes his own. —OLD MOGUL SPIRITUAL

*B*ecause childhood is a notoriously undercapitalized and powerless stage of human development, Moguls seldom have fond memories of it. In fact, most Moguls seem to have no memories of it at all.

Mogul Infant's "4 Years-at-a-Glance"

	9/84	3/85	6/85	9/86	3/86	9/87	9/88
Get born	X						
Sleep through night		X					
Talk		X					
Sit up		X					
Crawl		X					
Walk			X				
Hail cab		X					
Grab cup		X					
Grab spoon							
Feed self							
Smile							
Parallel play						X	
Play with others							
Get toilet-trained					X		
Make money						X	
Demand more money							

The Mogul Background

Despite popular misconceptions:

Moguls are not always Jewish.
Moguls were not all penniless immigrants.
Anyone with an insatiable drive to acquire money and power for
the primary purpose of amassing more and more of it can be a
Mogul . . . even middle-class Episcopalians.

Although the Mogul's roots are various, statistics compiled by the
Center for Advanced Mogul Studies indicate certain similarities in
Moguls' early development:

Born:
In a raging snowstorm 49%
In a barren desert waste . . 49%
Not sure 2%

Weaned:
Abruptly 100%
Gradually. 0%

First phrase:
"Give me" 56%
"I'm hungry" 43%
Other 1%

Favorite toy:
An adult★ 60%
Little sled with rosebud
    on it 30%
The telephone. 10%

First word:
"Me" 50%
"More" 50%

Attained puberty by:
6 years 83%
10 years 12%
"Before I can remember" . . 5%

Reached present height at:
10 years 98%
Other 2%

★ *Moguls dislike little children as much at four as they do at forty.*

A GIRL MOGUL'S MOTHER SHOULD SAY:

"We must do something about your (hair, nose, skin, nails, weight, posture, father)."

"Oh, was Christmas yesterday?"

AND A GIRL MOGUL'S DAD SHOULD SAY:

"Of COURSE I'll marry you, Princess."

"Good shot!"

"He's not good enough for you."

"Merry Christmas, Princess, your present's parked outside."

Parent Picks

IF YOU ARE A BOY MOGUL	IF YOU ARE A GIRL MOGUL

Your ideal father is:

1. Demanding, cold, never pleased with your accomplishments
2. Absent

Your ideal mother is:

1. Struggling to make ends meet by cleaning mean rich people's houses
2. Affectionate, demonstrative, proud of you
3. Dead

Your ideal dad is:

1. Dashing, handsome, erratic, flirtatious
2. Dead

Your ideal mother is:

1. Demanding
2. Jealous
3. In Europe

A BOY MOGUL'S DAD SHOULD OFTEN SAY:

"This morning he was 'your pet'; tonight he's dinner."
"Everything I have is yours, but you can't touch a cent of it until you're thirty-five."
"Little Runt."

A BOY MOGUL'S MOM SHOULD SAY:

"You're getting so big!"
"Don't get up, I'll get it for you."

5

MAKING THE MOGUL MIND

Poverty is life's cheapest lesson.
—MOGUL SCHOOLROOM SAMPLER

Mogul Elem. Ed.

Elementary school education provides a young Mogul with hands-on experience in the valuable fields of arithmetic, money management, and interpersonal manipulation. Here's a sample curriculum:

Learn to add.
Sell lunch.
Invest in white mice.
Learn to multiply.
Multiply mice.
Sell mice at profit.
With profit, pay class sneak-thief
    to steal test answers.
Sell test answers at profit.
Buy friends.

Mogul High

There are some things you need to learn in high school but not many:

MATH: Percentages
ENGLISH: Vocabulary
(But watch for misinformation. When they tell you *common* means
    crude, and *crude* means *uncouth*, REMEMBER: To a Mogul,
    common means *publicly issued stock*. *Crude* means *unrefined oil*.
    Time means *money*. *Five foot five* means *average*.)

SOCIAL STUDIES: Basic principles
The Territorial Imperative—"It's natural for Man to stake his
   claim to large blocks of real estate."
The Frontier Spirit—"Obey the Territorial Imperative."
Freedom—the right to exercise Frontier Spirit unimpeded by
   government regulation.
Rugged Individualism—Freedom.

Mog. U.

While a college degree is an invaluable asset in the business world,
a college *education* can be a serious liability, especially if overloaded
with Humanities. The Liberal Arts aren't called "liberal" for
nothing.

If you must go to college, use your time to make valuable business
contacts. All the academic knowledge you'll need in later life is
contained in the following . . .

MOGUL ETHICS:

It is morally wrong to allow suckers to keep their money.

MOGUL AESTHETICS:

Bigger is better.
More is more.

MOGUL POLITICS:

The Elephant is bigger than the Donkey (see "Aesthetics").

MOGUL PHYSICS:

What goes up, goes up still more after January.

MOGUL EPISTEMOLOGY:

Once you tell a thing three times, it's true.

MOGUL SEMIOTICS:

No one ever put out a sign that said, "Nice Dog."

Mogul History

ANTIQUITY:

10 million B.C.—Fire invented.

9.999 Mil. B.C.—Broiled steak invented.

2500 B.C.—Wheel invented.

2499 B.C.—Bigger wheel invented.

2498 B.C.—Chauffeur invented.

1300 B.C.—Moses receives world's first memo. Accepts first step-deal.

1241 B.C.—Egyptians invent the memo pad.

700 B.C.—Metal coinage introduced by Lydians to Asia Minor.

699 B.C.—Kickback invented by Asian minors.

688 B.C.—Percentage point invented.

336 B.C.—Alexander the Great, world's first Baby Mogul.

100–44 B.C.—Julius Caesar, world's first Global Mogul; first mogul to take meeting in bathroom; first Mogul to use real estate as dinner party conversation topic.

50 B.C.—Cleopatra, first Moguline, first to commit suicide to avoid corporate takeover.

A.D. 1—Years start running forward, progress invented.

33—Last Supper, first prototype of Testimonial Dinner.

330—Byzantine Empire founded, waiting room invented.

801—Charlemagne invents prayer breakfast.

1095–1291—The Crusades; first deductible business trip.

1174—Henry II does penance at Canterbury for murder of Becket; first mogul to get away with murder.

1206—Genghis Kahn, first official "Mongol" or "Mogul," begins career of loot, pillage, conquest.

1215—Magna Carta assures Moguls' privilege over kings'.

1264—Marco Polo becomes first superagent, with "Orient" as client. Invents working vacation.

1351—Stench of "Black Death" plague drives indoor tennis courts into open air.

1368—Ming porcelain becomes Moguls' first collectible.

1380—Clock tower invented; phrase "let's have lunch" sweeps Europe.

1492—American real estate discovered.

1513—Machiavelli writes *The Prince*, first official Mogul handbook.

1536—Calvin claims Moguls predestined for salvation.

MODERN TIMES (HIGHLIGHTS):

17th CENTURY:
The Age of Invention

Financial monopolies invented.
Bank of England founded; bank notes
invented.
National Debt invented.
Joint stock companies, insurance
companies, address books, letters of
credit and exchange invented.
Peter Minuit invents "sweetener
deal"; buys Manhattan from Indians
for $13 in beads, throws in $11 in
trinkets.

18th CENTURY:
The Enlightenment

Montesquieu comes out for limited
government.
Bentham invents Utilitarianism
("What makes more money for
moguls is good for moguls and
what's good for moguls is good").
Adam Smith coins term "Laissez-faire."
Marie ("let 'em eat cake") Antoinette
invents "trickle-down" theory.
Redcoats and Redskins conquered by
colonists.
Reason conquered by Man.

FREE
THE
FORBES
400

19th CENTURY:
The Age of Moguls

Herbert Spencer's interpretation of
  Darwin ("In nature, fittest survive")
  allows Moguls to enjoy nature.
Lincoln frees Southern Agrimoguls
  from having to feed excess slaves.
Karl Marx born, proved wrong, dies.
U.S. Steel wins Industrial Revolution.
Harrod's opens.
Today's Moët and Tattinger
  Champagnes begin fermenting.
John Jacob Astor invented.
Nature conquered by Man.

20th CENTURY:
The Age of More Moguls

Steam conquered by electricity.
Cottage industries conquered by
  assembly line.
Assembly line conquered by microchip.
Russian peasants duped into
  overthrowing Czar.
Hiroshima, Allende conquered by
  God's will.
Havana cigars become hard to get.
Women's liberation proved bad for
  girls, men.
Plastics, limos, Hollywood movies,
  digital LCDs, multinational
  corporations, Lear jets, thirty-second
  spots, fifty-minute hours, fallout
  shelters, tax shelters, computer graphics,
  cellular phones, low-cholesterol diets,
  and double-bypass surgery invented.
Environment discovered.
Frontier (west) closed.
New Frontier (poverty) closed.
Last Frontier (space) opened.
Man conquered by business.

Owning beats wanting.
Buying beats owning.
Making beats spending.
—OLD MOGUL ADAGE

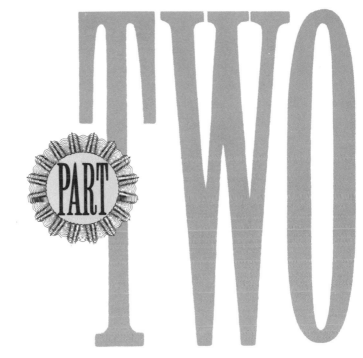

PART TWO

Getting

The minute you decide to be a Mogul, you must begin to amass your fortune. A Mogul Fortune begins "north of seventy." This means "upwards of seventy million dollars."

(Moguls don't use the word "million." To a mogul the word "million" is assumed to apply, unless billions are specified. In Dallas they don't use the words "one hundred million." The word "unit" is used instead.)

6

MAKING YOUR MILLIONS

Expand or die. —OLD JUNGLE LAW

As with many things Mogul, the general rule of thumb is: The Faster the Better.

Here are nine pretested Methods of getting over "the hump."

The One-minute Mogul

Strike Oil.
Or . . .
Corner oil.
Or . . .
Marry someone with oil.
Or . . .
Invent something better than oil.

The Two-step Plan

Go to country that has slavery.
Mine diamonds.

The Lo-skill Plan

Inherit vast fortune.
Increase vast fortune.
Shelter vast fortune.

Moguline Plan

Go to finishing school in Paris; buy nice clothes; speak softly;
   listen to men intently.
Marry American Mogul's son; become First Lady.
Marry Foreign Mystery Mogul; shun shutterbugs.

Mystery Mogul Plan

Leave Sicily for New York City.

Join cousin's funeral-parlor business.

Increase demand for funeral services.

Marry judge's daughter; send son to Yale; marry son to senator's daughter.

Change funeral business to parking-lot business.

Put nightclubs next to parking lots.

Buy entertainers.

Sell parking lots and nightclubs, buy small ailing movie studio.

Produce string of blockbusters.

Go public; retain major shareholder position; appoint son and former Secretary of State to board of new leisure corporation.

Buy and arm small Caribbean country for use as corporation golf course.

Build resorts, retirement communities on above.

Retire to Palm Springs.

Donate and deduct:
- a. Ophthalmology wing to UCLA Medical School
- b. 800-piece set of china to White House
- c. Correspondence with ex-Secretary of State to Harvard
- c. Son to U.S. Government (SEC, FCC, or Attorney General's Office)

Forget past.

The Master Builder Variant

Get born to father with run-down real estate in decaying city.

Improve properties by raising rents, turning neighborhood stores into boutiques and gourmet food shops, forcing unattractive poor people out of area.

Tell media you are "revitalizing the inner city."

Get tax break from city and borrow money to build luxury midtown tower designed by famous architect.

Name the tower after yourself.

Sell space at prices too high for anyone except rich foreigners to buy.

Tell media you are attracting fresh business resources to the Revitalized Inner City.

Get tax break from city and borrow money to revamp old hotel. Name it after yourself with word "Palace" added.

Form "I Love This City" group. Advertise it nationally.
Get more tax breaks, borrow more money, build more towers and
   hotels.
Hire wife's decorating company to redo the rooms.
Use wife in ad campaign.
Deduct wife.
Offer to take over construction of city's cost-overrun, long-
   delayed convention center, waterfront mall, and football
   stadium on condition that they be named after you.
Donate "vest pocket park" to ghetto.
Pick mayor.

Global Mogul Plan—Cannonball–Orient Express

Get born to wealthy Jews in Germany, ca. 1937.
Flee to France; learn French, wine, insouciance.
Emigrate to U.S. by age twelve.
After graduating from Harvard, go to Oxford as Rhodes Scholar,
   then the London School of Economics; buy Lobb's shoes;
   marry Queen Elizabeth's lady-in-waiting's niece; have blond
   children with British accents; return to U.S. by age twenty-five.
Work three months at Morgan Guarantee Trust; join clubs.
Become assistant to ancient chairman of brokerage firm; read his
   confidential memos and replace him.
Merge clients; take percentage of all mergers; use merged clients
   to take over rival firms' clients.
Save a state or city on brink of financial ruin, befriending
   Washington insiders in process.
Use Washington insiders' help to broker bigger mergers.
Become Professor Emeritus at Harvard; write book; give
   speeches.
Advise President of U.S.
Turn down cabinet post.
Become ambassador to nation that . . .
Has reliable
     a. air conditioning
     b. phone service
     c. airline

Suffers from
    a. weak army
    b. troubled borders
And needs
    a. low-paying jobs
    b. pipeline.
Avert coup.
Become Secretary of State; create brief cease-fire in Mideast; tap
    enemies' phones; manipulate press, recognize China.
Retire to St. Moritz; come out of retirement to serve on
    President's Commission.
Advise Socialist President of European country.
Shed last remaining trace of ethnic identity.
Create Annual Easter Egg Hunt with other post-ethnic Global
    Moguls.

The Red-White-and-Blue Method

Incorporate in Delaware.
Base in Houston.
Buy in Bukittinggi.
Design in Santa Clara.
Assemble in Seoul.
Appoint newly retired Joint Chiefs of Staff general to board.
Sell product to U.S. Armed Services.
Acquire companies which manufacture parts for product.
Subcontract parts from self.
Mark up.
Piggyback mark-ups.
Take ten years to make product.
Deliver obsolete product.

But surest of all is the old standby . . .

The Bernard Baruch Memorial Plan

Buy low.
Sell high.

7

MAKING MORE MILLIONS

> *Real wealth is a property of the mind.* —TED TUNA

*T*hough you're entitled to call yourself a Mogul after you're "over seventy" (million), no one else will. $150 mil is the minimum entrance requirement to the Forbes 400—the four hundred richest people in America—and any Mogul worth his/her portfolio will try to break into this club.

The simplest way to keep increasing your wealth is via the Leveraged Buy-Out or LBO. An LBO is a deal in which you borrow OPM (Other People's Money) to buy something which you can sell for more than you paid for it. This SUPER JAWS storyboard for the popular animated cartoon will show you how.

The Adventures of $uper Jaws

Wall Street's Flashiest Little Fish!

FRAME 1   Wall St. in background. River in foreground with shark fin visible.

Narrator: Faster than a futures trader! More powerful than CBS! Able to liquidate undervalued companies in a single buy-out! It's SUPER JAWS!

FRAME 2   Shark emerges from water, turns into an ordinary Mogul (Ted).

Narrator: . . . Who, disguised as Ted Tuna, mild-mannered venture capitalist of a great Metropolitan Holding Company, fights a never-ending takeover battle for cash! Power! and the American Way!

44

FRAME 3   Ted Tuna's lavish bedroom. Mermaids struggling to hold Ted in bed.

Mermaid #1: You can't Merge and Acquire all night!
Mermaid #2: Ted, you've got to get some rest!
Ted: No time! There's an undervalued company out there that needs me!

FRAME 4   Ted's huge office; Ted reading ticker tape.

Ted: Just as I thought! Conglamorex Inc. is selling at $35. It's got to be worth more! Put in an order for 5 percent of their stock!
Lackey #1: Only 5 percent?
Ted: Jerk, don't you know that if I buy more, I have to make a public announcement?

FRAME 5   EXTERIOR. Ted's office, Lackey #1 falling from window.

Ted (*in window, musing*): I wonder what kind of company Conglamorex is.

FRAME 6   Ted's office.

Lackey #2: Sir, their divisions include a movie studio, a paper mill, and a mining company, just like that other company you bought.
Lackey #3: You're in competition with yourself!
Ted: Great! I'll sell Conglamorex off for its real estate!

FRAME 7   Conglamorex Hdqrs.

CEO: Someone just bought 5 percent of us?!? WHO!?
Demi Panel: Associate whispers to CEO

FRAME 8   CLOSE UP of CEO, villainous.

CEO: All right, men, this calls for the poison pill!

FRAME 9   Floor of Stock Exchange.

1st broker: Conglamorex is at 38!
2nd broker: The rumor is, Super Jaws is after it.
1st broker: Let's get some—fast!

FRAME 10 Megafeller Bank—elegant, stuffy room.

Ted *(to bankers):* . . . So, as soon as you promise to lend me $600 million, I'll announce my intention to buy out Conglamorex.
Banker: We promise. No prob.

FRAME 11 Conglamorex Annual stockholders' meeting.

CEO *(to members):* . . . And to protect you shareholders from this hostile take-over bid we'll do everything we can to block Mr. Tuna!

FRAME 12 Stockholders.

Stockholder A: Our shares are worth $41 now, thanks to Mr. Tuna—not you!
Stockholder B: He says you've screwed up the company!
Stockholder C: Yeah!
Others: We need Super Jaws at the helm! Super Jaws! Super Jaws!

FRAME 13   Wall Street—buildings swaying.

Narrator: Rumors are rocking Wall Street.

FRAME 14   Men with bags over their faces.

Narrator: Anonymous sources say Ted Tuna has left for the Caribbean.

FRAME 15   Ted on yacht and Mermaids in water, helicopter above, from which CEO leaning out & throwing money:

CEO: Ted! Here's a hundred mil! Now leave us alone!
Ted: Getting rid of me's worth twice that! Buzz off!!

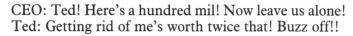

FRAME 16 Inside helicopter; CEO holds "poison pill," labeled "Anti-Takeover Law."

CEO: Quick! Drop this while his mouth's open.
Associate: Isn't that illegal?
Lawyer: No ruling on it yet.

FRAME 17 Yacht. Pill falls into Ted's mouth. He spits it out.

Ted: Ycch!

FRAME 18 CLOSE UP of Ted, furious.

Ted: Okay, you asked for it!

FRAME 19 Ted dives into the water — *"Splash!"*

FRAME 20 Natives on shore point to fin in water.

Native #1: Look! Down in de deep!
Native #2: It villain!
Native #3: It savior!

FRAME 21 CEO (in copter, sweating with dread!):

It's SUPER JAWS!

FRAME 22 Stockholders' meeting, SUPER JAWS in a big tank on dais beside sweating CEO.

Super Jaws *(inciting shareholders):* They offered me $60 a share, and yours are only worth $47!
Stockholder #1: That's Greenmail!
Many: Fire the board!!!

FRAME 23 Stockholders hold CEO over Jaws' tank.

CEO *(to Jaws):* Please! Please! We'll give you $1200 million! Just don't eat me!
Inset: CLOSE UP of Jaws, thinking: "Hmmm, double my potentially borrowed money back."

FRAME 24   Jaws *(to stockholders):* Lay off him, fellas, your shares are up to $52. We've all been fed.

FRAME 25   Wall Street ticker-tape parade. Placard-bearing throng shouting: Hooray for Jaws! He made MORE millions! One little kid: They PAID him not to borrow money??!?

8

KEEPING YOUR MILLIONS

... From the IRS.

> *Anyone can make money,*
> *but only the very rich can*
> *keep it.* —F. SCOTT FITZMOGUL

*I*t is every Mogul's tax goal to keep all his/her yearly earnings out of the public coffers while still appearing to be a patriot. You will find this relatively easy. The real challenge is explaining the apparent contradiction to *60 Minutes.*

Still, you must do something creative, because, left unchecked, the Feds will squeeze you dry, making up new rules the instant you figure out a way around the old ones. This Thumbnail Shelter Guide and Mogul Tax Return on the following page will help:

Guide to Tax Shelters

ALIMONY

Although paying alimony has the virtue of keeping the IRS's hands off your money, it has the drawback of keeping your hands off it too.

It is galling to sit helplessly watching one's ex-wife's shopping sprees on *Lifestyles of the Rich and Famous,* so, unless you are Johnny Carson and running low on comedy material, avoid paying alimony if possible.

CASH AND CARRY

This is the purchase of presold assets with borrowed funds. No one knows how it works, but many satisfied Moguls have discovered it does.

Mogul Tax Return—The Short Form

1986 GROSS INCOME: $15,000,000.00

TAX DEDUCTIONS

Alimony .... 1,181,222.05 (see "Alimony," below)

Capital losses
(to offset
capital gains).... 2,000,444.   (see "Widow" below)

Cash and carry .... 2,000,001.   (see "Cash and Carry,"
                                  below)

Equipment leasing . 1,999,999.   (see "Leaseback,"
                                  below)

Depreciation ...... 4,818,333.95 (see friendly
                                  congressperson)

Weird, dubious, new, risky
deduction your
accountant made   (if you can invest and
up .... 5,000,000.   double this amount
                                  before they (a) catch
                                  you, and (b) take you
                                  all the way up to the
                                  Supreme Court, it'll
                                  be worth it. Besides,
                                  they may not catch
                                  you at all.)

(TOTAL DEDUCTIONS: $15,000,000.00)

Net Taxable Income:
                    $ 00.00

(Needless to say, Moguls do not pay withholding.)

A WIDOW

If you have a lot of capital gains, you can shelter them by digging up a rich widow, one whose managers at American Trust have generously endowed her with lots of capital losses. Then:

1. Marry her on December 29.
2. File a joint return in which your gains are offset by her losses.
3. Divorce on January 4.
4. Split refund.

EQUIPMENT LEASEBACK

Borrow money from bank to buy computers. Lease computers back to bank (or someone else) for enough money to pay off the debt. Depreciate computers while paying for them. Get a big enough tax deduction on depreciation to offset cost of computers and end up with (in effect) free computers at end of lease.

IF ALL ELSE FAILS:

Buy island.
Declare independence.
Grant self citizenship.
Make self king or queen.
Tax islanders.
Get U.S. aid.

Make self king

9

YOUR EMPIRE

Edge, edge is everything.
—JIMMY THE GREEK

Profit, profit is everything.
—JIMMY THE MOGUL

*E*ighty percent of your time is spent enlarging your empire. Another 20% of your time is spent protecting it against envious, small-hearted people who try to shrink it.

I shop, therefore I am.
　　—DESCARTES'S WIFE

PART THREE

Spending

Once you've built an empire and put yourself on top of it, you're ready to prove your Mogul Mettle by spending your money in the Mogul Manner.

No matter how extravagant a Mogul's spending habits may appear, all Moguls spend money to make money. Every Mogul knows that . . .

Living Well Is the Best Deduction.

Moguls love to
Shop shop shop.
There's no need to
Stop stop stop.

Buy a country,

Buy a car,

Buy the building

Where you are.

Moguls love to
Shop shop shop.
There's no need to
Stop stop stop.

Buy some flowers,

Have them sent,

Buy the U.S.

government.

10

WHAT BECOMES A MOGUL MOST

Only God helps the badly dressed.
—SPANISH PROVERB

His Clothes

*S*artorially speaking, being a Male Mogul is like being a super-hero or a Hell's Angel—the outfit comes with the job. So if you're a guy who likes to "express your personality through your clothes," or a fashion addict with a yen for Japanese tweed, you'd be happier posing for *Uomo Vogue* than trying to pass for Uomo Mogul.

Her Clothes

Women make bankers nervous, but by flaunting her femininity in outfits by Adolpho, Chanel, or any name designer who lays "feminine" detailing (usually ruffles, frogs, decolletage or a cascade of jewels) on a firm foundation of classic tailoring, the Moguline evokes the image of an iron fist in a velvet glove. This reminds bankers of Bismarck, a person they trust.

Since the velvet-glove strategy works only for ladies with real wealth and power, it's easy to spot the difference between a Moguline and a Lady Exec.

Lady Exec	Moguline
Brooks Bros. Dress-for-Success suit	St. Laurent pinstripe Dress-for-Excess Suit
Cotton shirt, bow tie	Silk shirts
Gold earrings, single strand of pearls	Diamonds, pearl ropes
Bulky down coat	Maxmilian black mink or sable
Burberry trench	Silk raincoat
Running bra	Bra optional
Chanel #19	Own personal blend
Sensible pumps, Nikes for the commute	200 prs. Maud Frizon, Susan Bennis and Warren Edwards, Manolo Blahnik, Walter Steiger assorted shoes

Mogulines, when meeting with male Moguls, in deference to their colleagues' size, wear spikes only when provoked.

The Top Male Mogul
Costume No-No's

Sulka
Silk tie

NO coats. When it's cold, slip into your waiting limo. A coat bogs you down in the coat-check zone when you're party-hopping.

NO hats. Exceptions: If Texan, wear Stetson for riding. If not Texan, wear homburg to coronations.

NO money in pockets.

NO anything in pockets.

NO pockets on shirts.

NO buttonholes that don't work.

NO flowers in buttonholes; too French.

NO vests; too professorial.

NO corsets; too pathetic.

NO digital watches or nerd packs; too tech.

NO plaids; too prep.

NO epaulettes; too *Love Boat*.

NO fishnet or black leather anything with grommets.

NO bows on evening shoes.

NO Italian shoes (unless you're a Media Mogul).

NO moccasins or velvet slippers with little foxes on them (unless you're a Media Mogul).

NO gold chains (even if you are a Media Mogul).

NO cuff links made of unidentifiable metals or multicolored stones.

NO diamonds for day.

NO cummerbunds at night.

NO tie clips.

NO knit ties.

NO string ties (unless Western).

NO button-down shirts.

NO bikini anything.

NO anything with writing on it.

NO dirt under fingernails.

NO visible dandruff.

NO visible darning or reweaving.

NO visible facial hair.

NO false hair.

NO long hair.

NO short socks.

Real buttonholes

The Mogul Closet:

27 gray Pinstripe Suits

.5" stripe 6
1" stripe 12
1.5" stripe 5
2" stripe 4

45 Shirts with French Cuffs

20 white European Sea Island Cotton
10 blue European Sea Island Cotton
15 pinstripe in assorted colors
(gray and blue)

27 dark blue Pinstripe Suits

.5" stripe 6
1" stripe 12
1.5" stripe 5
2" stripe 4

45 Shirts with Two-Button Cuffs

20 white European Sea Island Cotton
10 blue European Sea Island Cotton
15 pinstripe in assorted colors
(gray and blue)

Tiffany gold knot cuff

Laces

Close shave

3" shirt collar

Three-letter monogram

Cartier watch

Inward pleats

Lobb's shoes handmade in London

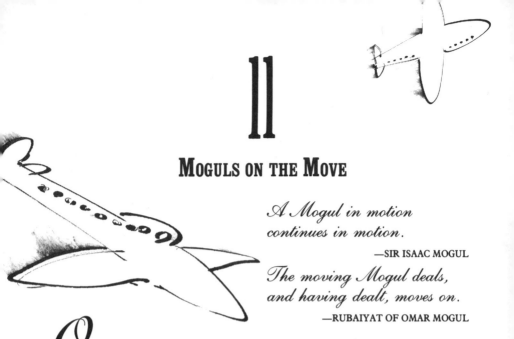

11

MOGULS ON THE MOVE

*A Mogul in motion
continues in motion.*

—SIR ISAAC MOGUL

*The moving Mogul deals,
and having dealt, moves on.*

—RUBAIYAT OF OMAR MOGUL

One never catches a Mogul leaning back against his/her limo, blowing lazily on a harmonica and singing:

> "I might take the bus;
> I might take the train;
> But if I have to walk,
> I'll get there just the same.
> Kansas City!
> Kansas City, here I come."

That's because Moguls don't . . .

1. Take the bus.
2. Take the train.
3. Walk.
4. Sing the blues.

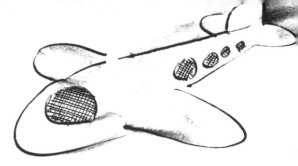

What a Mogul does do while traveling the Mogul Empire is to MAKE DEALS, so, once you're a Mogul, make sure you have cellular phones installed in all your vehicles.

Why Buy a Helicopter?

Even if you're not the kind of Mogul who visits his oil fields, vineyards, timberlands, beefalo ranches and uranium mines regularly, you should have a helicopter, preferably a Bell Jet Ranger piloted by a former Green Beret.

Arriving anywhere in a chopper is guaranteed to assert your power. Nothing makes as much noise, messes up other peoples' hair and lawns and puts them off balance as one of these numbers. Because people associate helicopters with heads of state and war zones, your ominous approach in one will scare the hell out of everyone and insure you a properly awed welcome.

Why Buy a Jet?

If you are a Mogul in Progress, you might question the wisdom of purchasing a plane, but consider . . . with a private jet you can:

Arrive in same city as your luggage.*
Meet with functionaries in-flight.
Exercise to reduce stress (bigger jets like a Gulfstream III,
    a BAC III, or a 727 only).
Take refreshing baths (ditto).
Smuggle.
Nap lying down.
Sit in cockpit with pilot.

---

* *To avoid refueling on your way to Europe, put luggage on your Lear and fly the Concorde.*

. . . and most important of all . . .

MAKE DEALS.

Close one solid deal over Climax, Colorado, and your plane pays
  for itself.

  IN OTHER WORDS, YOUR PLANE IS FREE.

As well as a valuable business tool, you'll find your jet a handy way
to impress guests.

Seven good excuses for inviting guests to ride in plane:

To watch your horse run in the Derby.
To watch your team play in the Superbowl.
To visit your yacht.
To visit your island.
The sun's out in Acapulco.
There's fuel in the jet.
The sun's out.

Your jet is not a toy, but properly used, it can be the next best
thing to a toy you've ever had.

  IN OTHER WORDS, YOUR PLANE IS FUN.

Finally, and most importantly, the private jet is one of the key
things which distinguishes Moguls from Non-Moguls.* Looked at
as a ticket of entry into the Mogul realm, it's cheap at any price.

---

* Except for Daniel Ludwig, who flies Economy.

Get two. The Lear is small, but a good beginner jet. A couple of them should get you where you're going no matter what. Only a Yogul would blow a deal because his jet broke down and he was too cheap to keep a backup.

Your Limo

"What do you decorate a car with?" "Black leather, chrome, and marble." "Why marble?" "For the sink and the hot-and-cold running-water bar."　　　　　　　　　　　—IVANA TRUMP ON LIMO DECORATION

Your limo is basically an office on wheels, with only two notable exceptions:
1. It's better for firing people. Just ask any lackey, exec, or other hireling to ride out to the airport with you. They'll instantly grasp that they're coming back by cab.
2. It's driven by a chauffeur. Hitler grew so fond of his chauffeur that he kept the man's photo beside his beloved mother's. Don't let anything that peculiar happen to you. Watch yourself: Don't get chummy. Stay on the phone.

Your Other Cars

Zen and the art of Rolls-Royce maintenance: Buy many valuable cars which will increase in value, but don't feel obliged to drive them. Remember:

Moguls are driven.

Others are taken for rides.

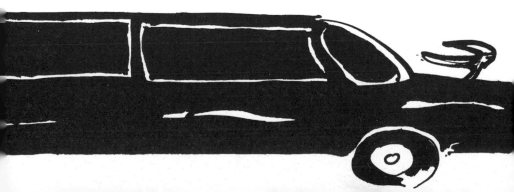

12

MOGUL HOMES

*In Xanadu did Genghis
Khan a lofty pleasure dome
decree . . .* —COLERIDGE

*A man's home is his castle,
but a Mogul's house is a real
castle.* —ANON.

*T*he Mogul house is less shelter than personal ornament, designed to enhance your prestige, glory, and deductible expenditures. Whether lush with Megalomogulian ostentation or as secretively exorbitant as an Upwardly Mogul's platinum Rolex, the Mogul home ALWAYS features:

Elbow room (it is huge).
Privacy (it is solid).
Architectural respectability (the architect is either famous or went to Yale).
High Resale value (no Non-Moguls in neighborhood).
75% T.D.

As a mogul, you must maintain at least three homes, of which at least one must be recreational.

Home Base for Texas and California Moguls
THE RANCH

Location: West of St. Louis, east of Eden, and bordering on a National Park
Size: Bordering on a National Park

Animals: Horses, preferably Polish-bred Arabian; cattle (inexplicably, sheep are too small for Moguls and pigs are not)

Purpose: To provide Mogul barbecue and pool with view, confirming Mogul identity

(View Rule: If you can stand on your roof and see someone else's property, you're NO MOGUL.)

Architecture: Roof low to the ground (see above) on sprawling "ranch house" in the Spanish Mission style, cool stucco labyrinth enclosing private courts vibrant with bougainvillea, rare flowering cacti, illegal alien help

The Mogul Ranch features:

Barbecue Pits—different ones for different-sized animals

Microwave barbecue pit—for rainy days when you're in a hurry

Nouvelle vegetable garden (California only)—For nights when you're tired of barbecue

Library—The complete works of James Michener (first editions) and a smattering of Louis L'Amour (signed), filled out with a leather-bound set of *The Reader's Digest* (heirloom) and *The Complete Ayn Rand* (paperback)

Media center—to entertain ranchers while waiting for library to become valuable

Game preserve—to have a place to put your satellite dish

Generator—so that air conditioning, Jacuzzi, and heating system for pool aren't knocked out in thunderstorms

Stable of polo ponies—to set an example for the other animals

Garage for jeeps—to set an example for the other cars

Sculpture garden (Texas only)—five acres, contemporary "conceptual" and earth works, to set an example for other Moguls

ARMED SATELLITE

WEATHER SATELLITE

MOUNT RUSHMORE (PROPOSED ADDITION)

SUGAR MOUNTAIN

ARTIFICIAL STURGEON & MISSILE

HELIPORT, RADAR STATION & BARRACKS FOR COUNTER-REVOLUTIONARY MILITIA

PERSONAL OPERA HOUSE AND BALLET COMPANY

HENRY MOORE SEATED NUDE

WINE

KENNELS FOR ATTACK DOBERMANS —GOOD FOR HANDLING PRESS.

MULTI-DENOMINAT. PRIVATE CHAPEL & BLUE VIDEO ARCHIVE

FAMOUS SUGGESTIVE TOPIARY GARDEN

CONSERVATORY CONTAINING ORCHIDARIUM AND THE ROSE GARDEN YOU NEVER PROMISED ANYBODY ELSE.

FOLLY CONCEALING ENTRY TO NUCLEAR SHELTER AND MUSEUM OF STOLEN ART

SURVEILLANCE SATELLITE

TV THEFT SATELLITE

CRISTO-WRAPPED MOUNTAIN

REPLICA OF MOUNT FUJI TO IMPRESS JAPANESE COMPETITORS

MONASTERY FOR (FREQUENT) RETREATS OF WIFE

...KE, ...TCHERY ...SE

OIL FIELD 50 YEARS RESERVE ...RDS ...AL

GENEROUSLY FUNDED FINISHING SCHOOL FOR YOUNG LADIES

THE ONLY REDWOOD YOU NEED EVER SEE

...URESQUE VILLAGE FOR SERFS

COTTAGE MOVED FROM NEWPORT

GARRET FOR CRAZY BROTHER (BARRED)

All-Purpose
Mogul Summer House

...AY FROM HERD OF ...ITE RHINOS ON ...D LIFE RESERVE

EARLY WARNING SATELLITE DISH

The TEXAS MOGUL must also keep a house in Houston, designed by the construction company that worked on the De Menils' Philip Johnson house, and one in Dallas, for weekend visitation with the kids.

The CALIFORNIA MOGUL must have a house in either Los Angeles or San Francisco, plus a beach house in Malibu, Hawaii, or Mexico and a full-sized apartment in New York.

California Mogul's City House

Northern California	Southern California
EXTERIOR	
Victorian	"Style" style. (Tudor Style, Spanish Style, Contemporary, Colonial, etc.)
INTERIOR	
Old Boston meets Gold Rush	Gidget meets Bauhaus
VIEW	
Alcatraz	Smog
REINFORCED AGAINST	
Earthquake	Earthquake, mudslides, nuclear war
CELLAR	
Wine (see "Your Wine Cellar" on page 95.)	Wine, granola (80 pounds), canned tuna (six months), Water (two months), Guns, ammo (nine months), Morphine (twelve months), Human hair wigs (1 per family member), Polygrip (life-time supply), map of stars' cellars

New York Mogul's House
THE NEW YORK (MANHATTAN) CO-OP

Dwelling size: A minimum of seventeen rooms
View of: Next state
Exclusivity ensured by:
1. Price
2. Co-op board, which rejects:
   a. the Nixons (plumbing risk)
   b. famous entertainers (security risk)
   c. anyone whose business is on Seventh Avenue (social risk)
   d. athletes (who'll be happier living near celebrities their own color)
   e. diplomats from emerging nations (all of the above)

The Country House

Location: Not too far (by helicopter) from Manhattan
Use: Thanksgiving
Decor: Consistent with the architecture of the period, i.e., looks like whichever rooms in the American Wing of the Metropolitan Museum of Art match your type of house.

The Beach House

Location: Not more than one hour from Manhattan by plane or two minutes from shoreline on foot.
House size: Visible from France
Property size: Four to seven party tents
Architect: White (Stanford)
Color: white (clapboard) or "weathered" shingles
Landscaping: Nonindigenous large trees from foreign countries
Decor: Ever-changing, from Rustic (French Provincial, English Proverbial, American Subsistence) to Overstuffed (vs. Italian) Modern, and back

Special Features
Separate guest quarters—Once a boathouse for a whaling fleet
Studio—For wife's artistic endeavors; once housing for migrant potato pickers
Gazebo—once a lighthouse

Pool house—once a windmill
Pool—once a duck pond
Artificial pond—once wetland
Tennis court—once a potato field
Nature preserve—once Nature
Fireplaces—for the one cold night each summer
Air conditioning—for the one hot day each summer
Dune—built up with scrap metal to stop beach erosion
Jetty—to direct erosive tides onto neighbor's property
Water—Mogul walks to water's edge twice a year to see if tides
     have added to property. This is called "going in the water," as
     in "We've been going to the beach weekends, but I haven't
     gone in the water yet."
Ocean—Moguls never go in the ocean.

The Midwestern Mogul's House

Just like the New York Mogul except:
A Midwestern Mogul's main house is the country house.
A Midwestern Mogul's beach house is a yacht.

(A SOUTHERN MOGUL is like a Midwestern Mogul except
a Southern Mogul's beach house is an island off the Carolina coast.)

Since Moguls don't pack, each house should be suitably equipped
as well as fully staffed (in season).

You will also require:

A Pied-À-Terre

. . . in any city you frequent on business. The last thing you need
in a foreign city is to feel foreign.

Take a permanent suite at the Pierre or Carlyle in New York, a
private bungalow at the Beverly Hills or Bel Air Hotel in Los
Angeles, a leisurely idyll at $500 a night in the Fairmont Suite in
Dallas, or make special arrangements in anything called the Ritz-
Carlton.

13

ANDY
WARHOL

THE FINE ART OF MOGULDOM

*Beauty is in the eye of the
Beholden.* —CHARLES REVSON

he Art bug bites Moguls of all types. When it bites, Moguls, aided by curators, gallery dealers, critics, and art historians, amass brilliant Art collections.

You will find your many homes an ideal stopover zone for your Art on its journey from prestige auction house to museum, where, in exchange for a tax deduction, you will bequeath your collection to posterity. In the meantime, photographs of paintings from your collection make great Xmas cards.

JULIAN
SCHNABEL

GREAT
COLLECTORS

GEORGE
SEGAL

Choose your art-buying style from one of the standard Mogul models:

New York Moguls

. . . buy art as an investment in America's cultural superiority over the Communist world. They therefore . . .

Own at least one important religious relic from a religion not their own (proving tolerance).

Dream of issuing limited reproductions of their collection to the public and making a fortune (proving opportunity).

NEW YORK MOGULS hang their collections in three or more sections:

The Manhattan apartment:
French Impressionists,* religious relics, English oils of bloody kills.

"The Beach":
a. Modern classics—Larry Rivers, Milton Avery, Keith Haring. Respecting the "asthetic of impermanence" in modern painting, Moguls hang modern art works in the ocean air, where corrosion adds poignance to their beauty.
b. Sculpture—Henry Moore.

Other Houses:
Art in New York Moguls' other houses should include (a) Rauschenbergs or Schnabels, (b) miniature replicas of Mogul's Henry Moores.

California Moguls

. . . buy art as an investment in their city's ability to compete culturally with New York.

---

* *Moguls consider Dufy an Impressionist.*

Art in Beverly Hills or Bel Air House:
American. Remington (cowboy bronzes and round-up paintings) or modern, specifically: one de Kooning (vagina dentata series); one Hockney; one Ed Ruscha; one bronzed TR-3 (son's first sports car); one John Chamberlain sculpture (made from son's first sports-car wreck); one Running Fence (after Christo via Richard Serra) designed by wife, blocking view of garden from Sunset Blvd.; and two white convertibles (one Packard and one Stutz) on blocks in the garage. Some French Impressionists.
Art in Malibu Beach house: A Warhol "Marilyn" litho. Daughter's self portrait on mirror from art class. Son's painting of "Tall man with stick (daddy)" from third grade. Wife's postmodernist wax-and-acrylic triptych: "Melon Wedges with Prosciutto Beset by Wasps."

California Mogul's New York corporate apartment: Rembrandt etchings, "Scenes from the Life of Christ" (charged to business).

Boston Moguls

. . . buy art as an investment in Bostonian tradition, and so . . .

collect Sargent, Whistler, Mary Cassatt, and Giotto.

Great Whites

. . . buy art as an investment in their own public image. So a Great White . . .

commissions bronze statue of self engaged in favorite sport (quail shooting, racquetball) to be erected in front of company gym.

All Other Moguls

. . . buy art as an investment, period.

No Moguls

No Moguls collect Duchamps.

14

MERGERS AND ACQUISITIONS

. . . For richer or richer . . .

—PART OF MOGUL MARRIAGE CEREMONY

*M*oguls have so little time to spend with their families that only a dynasty provides a Mogul's loved ones with enough company and attention to make it through life with a Mogul. Since creating a dynasty takes years, most Moguls marry young.

The Marrying Mogul

Marriage is good for Moguls. It provides them with the one confidante who can't be forced to testify against them in court.

If you're a male Mogul, a wife can be your greatest asset, displaying your incredible wealth by wearing clothes and jewelry you can't, extending your sphere of influence into social and cultural realms which bore you, and remembering your childrens' names.

Mogul Courtship (His)

Alas, while being married is wonderful for Moguls, courting—which entails being vulnerable—is not; so Moguls have evolved an oblique style of courtship. A woman who is true Mogul Mate Material will recognize your good intentions immediately if:

You remember her name.
You show up at least once every month.
You don't introduce her to other Moguls.
You have her phone tapped.
You pay off her current boyfriend.
You buy her an art gallery or boutique.
You ask for the name of her attorney.

Mogul's Prospective Wife (Checklist)

Happily, finding a spouse is easy, if you know what to look for:

Can she . . .
- [ ] Make Inferiors feel appreciated?
- [ ] Make Inferiors feel inferior?
- [ ] Make other Moguls feel tall?
- [ ] Distinguish a Louis XV armoire from a reproduction?
- [ ] Read ticker tape?
- [ ] Read?
- [ ] Read you?
- [ ] Speak Spanish to the maid?
- [ ] Speak Doublespeak to the press?
- [ ] Get dressed in 15 minutes?
- [ ] Table a personal question for fifteen years?

Is she free of . . .
- [ ] Cellulite?
- [ ] Unsightly Body hair?
- [ ] Moods?

Will she someday be capable of figuring out . . .
- [ ] When it's time for you to take your heart pill?
- [ ] Which house your Schlumberger lapis cufflinks are in?
- [ ] Which school(s) the children have been sent to?

Lastly, is she . . .
- [ ] Optimistic?
- [ ] Attractive?
- [ ] Elegant?
- [ ] Sociable?
- [ ] Diplomatic?
- [ ] A good organizer?
- [ ] A good sport?
- [ ] A great listener?
- [ ] Available?
- [ ] Undersexed?
- [ ] Grateful?

Mogul Courtship (Hers)

1. Either
   a. meet a man who reminds you of your father, or
   b. have your father introduce you to someone who reminds him of himself.

Mogul Divorce

Most Moguls enjoy long, enduring marriages. Divorce is financially distasteful and fairly easy to avoid. You spend so little time around your house(s), you can table differences with a spouse indefinitely. Still, a Mogul isn't afraid to cut his/her losses if a mate isn't working out.

GROUNDS FOR MOGUL DIVORCE

You're a Megalomogul and your wife joins an ashram.
You're an Upwardly Mogul and your wife says "oy vey."
You're a Foreign Mogul and your wife allows herself to be
    photographed with the kids.
You're a Mystery Mogul and your wife talks.
You're a Hollywood Mogul and your wife starts to remind you of
    your mother.
You're a Moguline and your husband stops reminding you of
    your father.
You're a Global Mogul and your wife gets jet lag or isn't
    Episcopalian (and you meet someone who is).
    Your wife announces she
        intends to age
        naturally.

IDEAL MOGUL DIVORCE

Restore cathedral.
Have audience with Pope.
Get annulment.

GENERIC MOGUL DIVORCE

Put all money into Union Banque Suisse or Cayman Islands.
Send mistress/lover on vacation to Acapulco (foreign country with
    favorable exchange rate).
Sell last two Rollses. File personal bankruptcy.
Pay off wife's (a) lawyer, (b) psychiatrist, (c) household help.
File papers.
Buy judge.

Typical Mogul's Typical Wife's Typical Day

7:00– 7:30	Breakfast with Mogul.[1]
7:30– 8:00	Order household help around.
8:00– 9:00	Take nap.
9:00–10:00	Talk on phone with Dominick Dunne.
10:00–11:30	Hairdresser appointment.[2]
11:30–12:30	Fitting at Adolpho's.[3]
12:30– 2:30	Lunch at Mogul Wife's restaurant[4] with other Mogul Wives or Jerry Zipkin.
2:30– 3:30	Facelift.
3:30– 4:30	Committee meeting to plan benefit for terminal-disease[5] research.
4:30– 4:45	Visit jewelry[6] in vault.
4:45– 5:00	Visit decorating business[7] (financed by husband)
3:30– 5:00	Shop (alternate days).
5:00– 6:00	Home for appointments with exercise instructor and masseur.
6:01– 6:11	Quality time with children.
6:02– 6:11	Bathe and feed dogs.
6:12– 7:00	Bathe and dress self.
7:00– 8:00	Attend cocktail party in honor of out-of-town Mogul.
8:00–11:00	Attend charity ball for terminal disease.[5]
11:00–11:30	Pamper mogul.
11:30–	Take sleeping pill.

---

[1] *Betsy Bloomingdale skipped this, with sad results.*

[2] *In NYC, Elizabeth Arden, Kenneth, Suga;*
in Houston, Hair Masters; in St. Louis,
Tommy's; in Los Angeles, home.

[3] *Or Oscar de la Renta, or Bill Blass.*

[4] *In NYC, Le Cirque, La Côte Basque, Mortimer's; in L.A., Ma Maison.*

[5] *Or any disease Moguls and their wives might get.*

[6] *Must include: Tiffany diamond ring (10 carat min., certified by American Gemologi-cal Institute); gold Cartier watch (with engraved inscription from Mogul on back); diamond and sapphire earrings, VanCleef and Arpels; diamond and ruby earrings, Harry Winston; mother-of-pearl earrings, Seaman Scheppes; Bulgari antique coin necklace; David Webb lion bracelet; diamond choker from 47th Street.*

[7] *Or art gallery.*

Qualities of Women in Mogul's Life

1ST WIFE	2ND WIFE	MISTRESS
Wide hips	No hips	Infertile
Heroine is: Eleanor Roosevelt	Heroine is: Babe Paley	Heroine is: Jerry Hall
Wears: Mink	Wears: Sable	Wears: Harem pants
Runs: Mogul's House	Runs: part of Mogul's empire	Runs: eight miles per day
Favorite singer: Frank Sinatra	Favorite singer: Julio Iglesias	Favorite singer: Linda Ronstadt
Watches *Dynasty*	Watches *Dynasty*	Watches *Dynasty*
Reads *Vogue*	Reads French *Vogue*	Works out
Felt sorry for: Betsy Bloomingdale	Felt sorry for: Cristina De Lorean	Felt sorry for: Vicki Morgan

Mogul wife between 5:00 and 5:15

Atypical Mogul's* Typical Wife's Typical Day

Dawn–6:00   Wake up. Swim 40 laps.
6:00 A.M.–10:30 P.M.   Run biz. Kick ass.
10:30–11:00   Debrief Mogul.
11:00–11:30   Scheme.
11:30   Sleep.

The Mogul Mistress

Only a minority of Moguls keep mistresses. A lack of time, a waste of money, fear of blackmail, germs, and the specters of various Kennedy mistresses are some of the reasons. In choosing a mistress, the wise Mogul checks her résumé for evidence that (a) she is emotionally self-sufficient; (b) she has had a rich boyfriend whom she did *NOT* take to the cleaners; and (c) that she's a bit too scattered to find the cleaners even if she wanted to.

A Typical Mogul's Typical Mistress' Typical Résumé

"Communicator" with diversified international exposure. Well versed in most areas of media/recreation interface. Seeks position with independent film production company.

---

* *Mostly Real Estate and Great White Moguls. This is also a Moguline's typical day.*

PHOTOGRAPHY
Photographer: Revival Publications Inc. N.Y.C. (Spring, 1985)
- Photographer assigned to article, "The Many Moods of Jerry Hall" for mock-up of proposed: *The New Yellow Book* magazine.

Photographer: The Turkish Government, Istanbul. (1979)
- Photographed storyboard for a series of 3 one-hour specials on the Middle Ages entitled (in rough translation) "The Good Old Days."

Photographer: Panama Airlines, Panama (1978–79)
- Solely assigned to photograph "old and new" Central America for travel poster campaign to promote tourism.
- Wrote copy for all photographs.

Assistant Photographer: The Nature of Nature Productions, Ltd. Jakarta/ Hong Kong (1977–78)
- Participated in efforts of photographic crew to film two feature-length documentaries to be distributed in sixty-three countries—*To Know a Rhino* (the Punjab) and The *Very Private Life of the Orang-Utan* (Ngabang, Borneo).

ADMINISTRATIVE
Administrative Director, Shangri-La Tours Ltd., Bali (1980)
- This unique family business catered to international celebrities as well as professional botanists and horticultural experts from Istanbul to London.

RESEARCH/MARKETING
Researcher: For Nonesuch Press, Inc. (1976)
- Traveled throughout Peru conducting in-depth research on level of English spoken, thereby evaluating potential markets in all sectors.

GENERAL BACKGROUND
Moved to London, England, (1981–85). Held positions as:

Interior Decorator (freelance)	Model (freelance)
Spotter for Christie's	Riding Instructor

EDUCATION
Graduated U. Miami, Fla. B.A. F.A. (1975)
Jakarta Highlands Secretarial/Finishing College, Jakarta. (certificate) (1976)

LANGUAGES IN ADDITION TO ENGLISH

Some Indonesian	French (passable)
Spanish (some)	

References upon request

Mogul mistress
before
meeting Mogul

The Mogul's Parents

The Mogul's parents get on the Mogul's nerves. They remember the Mogul in embarrassing situations—like childhood —and may even want to take some credit for his success. Sometimes the Mogul disowns his parents altogether, claiming to have been an orphan, but usually the Mogul buys them a house in Florida and visits them once a year. If the Mogul's father is rich, the Mogul has to be richer and beat the father in gin rummy, or golf, or in getting things named after him.

The Mogul's Siblings

Moguls like their brothers to be priests or doctors. An occasional Mogul will share his empire with a younger brother, provided the younger brother idolizes him and is willing, if necessary, to go to jail for the Mogul. A Mogul's sisters, like Napoleon's, cause nothing but aggravation.

The Mogul's Brother-in-law

If he has money of his own, the brother-in-law will be invited to invest it in one of the Mogul's riskier schemes. If poor, the brother-in-law is put to work in

a humiliating capacity within the empire, serving as a constant reminder to the rest of the family of the Mogul's generosity.

The Mogul's Nephew

Moguls often send their nephews to law school and then retain them for life—at a discount rate. By constantly comparing a son unfavorably with a nephew, Moguls are often able to increase their sons' productivity. When necessity demands it, nephews are also a great tool for driving a Mogul's son completely and terminally crazy.

The Mogul's Relatives

For aunts, uncles, cousins, nieces, and in-laws who have never tried to borrow money from the Mogul, it's an invite to Mogul family weddings, bar mitzvahs, etc. For those who have tried to borrow money, it's their funeral.

The Mogul's Son-in-law

The son-in-law is given a meaningless but tiring job in the empire so that the Mogul can keep an eye on him. Son-in-law is handy butt of Mogul jokes when brother-in-law is on vacation.

The Mogul's Children

Moguls are devoted to their children, eager to help name them, and quick to donate money to their chosen schools. Moguls become so attached to their children that when the children grow up and become capable of leading their own lives, the Mogul sulks. The smart Mogul's aim in child-rearing is to avoid such a moment. Just follow a few simple rules:

1. SPOIL the young child (lavish with all that money can buy).
2. DEPRIVE the grown child (never give him/her enough to make it without you).
3. CRUSH the first child who challenges your power as an example to the others.

Of course you want your children to achieve, but it must be understood that success does not mean succession. Only Yoguls hand over their empires while they can still pick up a phone. Instead, use the "Gotcha!" maneuver, in which you . . .

1. Hand empire over to son.
2. *Spring* out of retirement and oust him.

This is not only a rejuvenating experience for you, it is a fine learning experience for the boy, and clever Moguls swear by it.

In these modern times, you're well advised to treat daughters much as you would sons, except, of course, that a daughter must be able to count on her Mogul parent in any serious crisis:

SERIOUS CRISIS	MOGUL'S SOLUTION
Daughter dates headline writer for the *New York Post*	Mogul gets Rupert Murdoch to promote writer to editor of *The Australian Times*
Daughter falls in love with Afro-American terrorist.	Mogul gets daughter out of jail; marries her off to her bodyguard.
Daughter gets pregnant by married Greek shipping magnate.	Mogul pays for wedding.

Pets

There are only two kinds of pets suitable for a Mogul:
1. Dogs
2. Polish-bred Arabian horses

The only real qualification for a Mogul's dog is its complete devotion to the Mogul—even though the animal is fed, walked, and groomed (except for baths; see "Mogul's Wife's Day," above) by the chauffeur.

Mute and loyal, a dog is an unbeatable companion for a Mogul, but it cannot, however pedigreed, pack the financial punch of an Arabian steed. Though not cheap to buy, an Arabian can be depreciated over three to five years. Its upkeep is deductible, and if you get bored with it, you can sell it at a glamorous, celebrity-packed (also deductible) auction for as much as three mil, with profits from the sale taxed as capital gains at 20% max. This, clearly, is a pet you can talk to. And understand.

15

THE SOCIAL MOGUL

*It's my party
And I'll do what I want to.*

—MOGUL HIT SONG OF THE '50S

$\mathcal{T}$raditionally, social life is rife with business opportunities, so you will want to have a rich one, full of potential investors and the celebrities who attract them. This quest will take you to events such as:

A cruise on Malcom Forbes's yacht, the *Highlander*
Iriving ("Swifty") Lazar's Academy Award party
Summer camp at Bohemian Grove
An intro to Prince Charles and Princess Di at J.C. Penney

But no matter how glamorous your social whirl, you'll always prefer:

Entertaining at Home

Moguls prefer entertaining at home to going out, because *chez* Mogul:
1. You can show off your houses and collections.
2. You know where the phones are.

As the Host, however, you'll have to carry the conversational ball or risk being bored. Don't worry about boring *them*. In the hopes of picking up a stray business tip, most guests will hang upon your every other word.

ACCEPTABLE TOPICS FOR MOGUL PARTY CHAT

1. Autobiography
   a. acquisitions
   b. achievements
   c. philosophy
2. Forecasts
   a. interest rates
   b. economic rebound
   c. the weather

Note: If someone asks you about a book, avoid the temptation to boast that you don't have time to read books. Instead, call all literature "fiction" and say, "I haven't read any fiction since college."

PARTY GAMES

Moguls are not fond of party games. Still, when you get tired of talking, a game of backgammon offers a profitable alternative. If you are married to a renegade WASP, she may try to relax your guests by initiating a game like charades or Find the Fabergé Egg, but only—with luck—on special occasions. Better entertainment by far is THE HOUSE TOUR, which should always include:

Your Wine Cellar

Highly Visible
'18 Latour
'29 Lafite Rothschild
'37 Haut-Brion
'45 Mouton Rothschild
'45 Cheval Blanc
'67 Château Yquem

For the Table

CHAMPAGNE

'71 Dom Pérignon—3 cases
'75 Dom Pérignon—5 cases

RED BORDEAUX

Yr	Label	# Cases
'61	Haut-Brion	3
'61	Lafite Rothschild	5
'66	Lafite Rothshild	5
'66	Mouton Rothschild (label too avant-garde)	1
'71	Latour	5
'71	Cheval Blanc	1

WHITE BURGUNDIES

Yr	Label	# Cases
'75	Montrachet	7
'79	Bâtard-Montrachet	4
'79	Corton-Charlemagne	3

CALIFORNIA CABERNET SAUVIGNONS

Yr	Label	# Cases
'68	Mondavi Reserve	4
'74	Heitz Martha's Vineyard	4
'78	Jordan	10
'78	Stag's Leap	4
'78	Caymus Reserve	3

CALIFORNIA CHARDONNAYS

Yr	Label	# Cases
'78	Stony Hill	5
'78	Chateau St. Jean	3
'79	Chalone	7
'79	Villa Mt. Eden	3
'80	Acacia	7

Your Private Screening Room

A movie your megacorp produced or on which you personally lost money is always acceptable entertainment if screened in your private screening room. Other people's movies are sometimes permissible, but be careful what you show. Hollywood lefties deliberately make titles confusing.

YOU MAY SHOW	AS OPPOSED TO
Patton	*Potemkin*
Superman	*Superfly*
Mr. Billion	*Mr. Mom*
Ben Hur	*Ben Gurion Remembers*
Barbarella	*Julia*
Ten	*Nine to Five*
The Last Tycoon	*The Last Hurrah*
Red River	*Reds*
Star Wars	*WarGames*
The Empire Strikes Back	*The Empire of Passion*
The Sting	*The Swarm*
The Wrath of Khan	*The Grapes of Wrath*
For a Fistful of Dollars	*F.I.S.T.*
For a Few Dollars More	*Dollars ($)*
Raiders of the Lost Ark	*Lost Horizons*
The Godfather	*The Gods Must Be Crazy*
Anything with John Wayne	Anything with Alan Alda
High Noon	*High Anxiety*
Daughter's college film project	*Citizen Kane*
Your home movies	*Ordinary People*

16

FOOD FOR MOGULS

Never eat more than you can lift.
—MISS PIGGY

*T*here are those who eat to live, and those who live to eat, but the Mogul is neither. The Mogul meal is primarily a social occasion, designed to fuel deal-makers while deals are made.

Still, even Moguls have individual tastes. These tend to be either the foods they grew up on or the foods they grew up unable to afford. When you entertain at home, always have your kitchen staff prepare those foods you like best.

Moguls Like
Fresh-squeezed orange juice
Wheaties
Bacon and eggs
Creamed spinach
New York cut steak with
    fried potatoes
Meat (barbecued)
Birds (stuffed)
Fish (no heads)
Lobster
Smoked salmon
Beluga caviar
"Sauce on the side"
Hershey bars with almonds
Coffee ice cream

Moguls Don't Like
Mango-papaya cocktail
Kippers
Granola
Arugula
Sprouts (alfalfa, bean, or
    brussels)
Goat
Crow
Conch
Sea urchin
Lox
Stuffed zucchini blossoms
Zitti in brodo
Yogurt
Anything with pits

MYSTERY MOGULS LIKE: Pizza, Chinese food (Sunday night only)

GLOBAL MOGULS AND MOGULINES LIKE: Chinese food (in China).

BABY MOGULS LIKE: Everything except spinach and liver.

Going Out

When you must go out, you will have to adapt your tastes to those of the other Moguls with whom you will be dining.

THE BUSINESS BREAKFAST

Object: Cost efficiency
Menu: Black coffee, fresh orange juice, bacon and eggs
Locations: Regency and Carlyle Hotels, NYC
            Peachtree Plaza and Omni, Atlanta
            Loewe's Anatole, Dallas
            Stanford Court, S.F.
            Beverly Hills Hotel, L.A.

THE PRAYER BREAKFAST

Object: To obtain government contract
    (the only time moguls have been known to kneel)
Menu: Buttered biscuits, aged smoked ham, red-eye gravy
Location: Conference room

LUNCH AT THE CLUB

Object: To mix with money
Menu: Mixed grill
Location: Brook Club, Links Club, Downtown Assn., NYC
      Pacific Union Club, Bohemian Club, S.F.
      Duquesne Club, Pittsburgh
      Capital City Club, Atlanta
      California Club, Los Angeles
      Noonday Club, St. Louis
      Chicago Club, Chicago
      Petroleum Club, Denver
      Petroleum Club, Tulsa
      Oil Club, Houston

LUNCH AT THE SPORTS CLUB

Object: To mix with other Moguls
Menu: Chef's salad
Location: Yours or theirs

THE ALL-MOGUL DINNER

Object: To celebrate the success of an all-Mogul investment scheme
Menu: Beef Wellington, Baked Alaska, old Lafitte, Havana cigars
Location: Private room in Mogul restaurant or club

THE TESTIMONIAL DINNER

Object: To receive praise
Menu: Fish in aspic, glazed meat, melon balls and sherbet, warm
   wine
Location: A dais

THE BENEFIT DINNER DANCE

Object: To placate wife
Menu: Fish in aspic, glazed meat, melon balls and sherbet, warm
   wine
Location: Ballroom or cultural institution closed off from the
   public with thick red velvet ropes

Object: To have dinner at the White House

The Mogul Restaurant

One of the pleasures of being a Mogul is having your own great table at a restaurant. You get this table by buying it—like a co-op —and paying monthly maintenance on it.[1] Qualities of a Mogul restaurant:

Moguls get all the best tables.[2]

It's named after the owner, as in: Antoine's (Atlanta, New Orleans); Anthony's (St. Louis); Chasen's (L.A.); Jack and Charlie's "21" (NYC); Murray's Steak House (Minneapolis); Ernie's (S.F.)[3]

The prices are insane.

The menu is in English.

The food won't kill you.

There's a clearly marked ghetto[4] for Non-Moguls.

It's not a fad.[5]

HINTS:

Get the menu with prices on it. To a Mogul, the price of a dish is half its flavor, so let your guests savor it, too.

Don't carry money. Have your bill sent to your office (the service is always included).

Never reach for the bill and say: "What's the damage?"

---

[1] *See first item p. 108.*

[2] *That's why Elaine's is not a Mogul restaurant, even though it has all of the other prerequisites for being one.*

[3] *There are a few Mogul Restaurants not named after their owners: L.A., the Bistro; NYC, Le Cirque; Chicago, Perroquet; Dallas, Mansion at Turtle Creek; Philadelphia, The Frog*

[4] *Called Siberia.*

[5] *Moguls don't try new restaurants.*

17

MOGUL R & R

All work and no play makes a lot of jack. —MOGUL SECRET

*B*ecause no one really understands that Moguls' favorite form of recreation is work, doctors and loved ones are always pressuring you to RELAX. Every once in a while to get these people off your back you must endure "leisure," which often means taking a vacation.

Travel Tips

For TOURING, stick to the U.S. and Great Britain, avoid foreign countries. Foreigners don't appreciate all America's done for them, and many haven't even bothered to learn English.

For RESORTS, go to countries where they still know the value of good service:

Casa de Campo, Dominican Republic
La Samana, St. Maarten
Mill Reef Club, Antigua
Hotel du Cap, Antibes, France
Your private estate, your private island

To find an appropriate resort, have your secretary or wife ask the travel agent:

Is it expensive enough?
Is the beach long and white?
Is there a phone by the pool?
Is the airstrip long enough for a Lear?
Are there jellyfish?

Is the water safe to drink?
Is that guy who won at Wimbledon still the tennis pro?
What time does the *Wall Street Journal* arrive?
Are there walls/guards to keep out rebels?
Do you have a backup generator?

Leisure Activity

To avoid boredom on vacations, choose stressful pursuits providing you with: bloodshed (hunting, fishing); physical danger (skiing, yachting): unbridled competition (tennis, polo, horseracing); and financial swordplay (gambling, golf).

GOLF

This is your favorite sport because it provides you with the best cover for doing deals while on vacation.

TENNIS

Moguls play tennis much like other tycoons except a True Mogul keeps his/her own pro on full salary. While it's the pro's rare privilege to beat the Mogul at this game, the pro's main job is to serve the Mogul balls.

YOUR YACHT

Only Yoguls have sailboats. Moguls have power yachts.

The classic choice: An old Stevens or a Trumpy.
Over 100 feet: Fead ships are best.
Over 200 feet: Commission from shipyard.
> Features: For fast day trip from Miami to Bimini or Cat Key for fishing, carry aboard a Magnum or Riva speedboat, or, for longer trips, a customized Rybovich fishing boat with digital electronics and an elevator to the tuna tower.

> Yacht must have redundant systems: ship-to-shore telephone *and* Telex. Radar, sonar, VHF, SSB radios, satellite navigation system, life preservers, depth charges, weatherfax, seawater purification system, helipad.

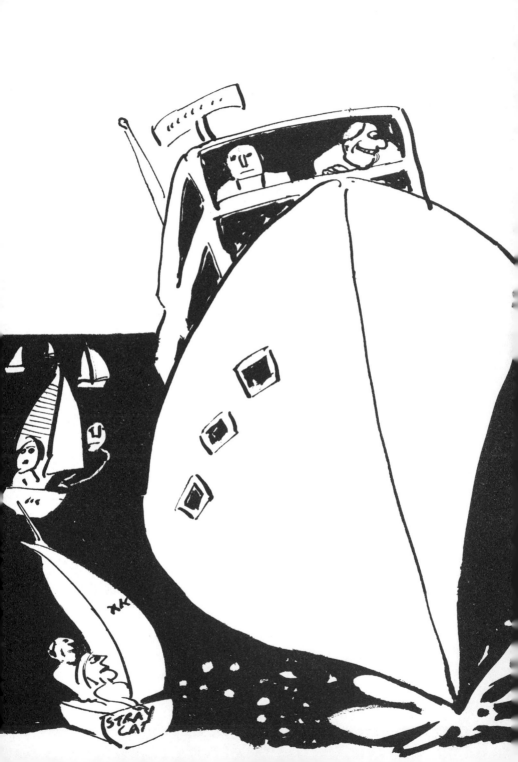

Yacht also needs valuable paintings, an Olympic pool, solid-gold-and-lapis bathroom fixtures, a uniformed crew, a personal flag, and flag of small, tax-free country in which boat is registered.

Once yacht is purchased and outfitted:
Name it after daughter or empire.

Keep yacht in port near airstrip. Put family on yacht; fly in for the night (or not).

PERMISSIBLE YACHT CLUBS

Palm Bay Club
Jockey Club
Boca Raton Club
Ida Lewis
Marblehead Yacht Club

Seewanaca Yacht Club
Los Angeles Yacht Club
Newport Harbor Yacht Club
New York Yacht Club
79th St. boat basin, NYC

HUNTING

Hunt regularly:
Wild Duck, with Purdy 12-gauge, in Maryland
Quail, with Holland and Holland 20-gauge, in Georgia
Fox, with Mannlicher-Schoenhauer .30-30 in Virginia

Recall aloud having once hunted:
Big mammal (e.g., polar bear) with Mauser .44 magnum with a
    4X scope in Africa or on solo Arctic safari.

FISHING

Moguls score 100% on this Easy Mogul Fishing Test. Match the
five fishes with their appropriate locations and bait:

Fish	Location	Bait
Scotch salmon	Scotland	Dry fly
Marlin	Bahamas	Smaller fish
Brook trout	Colo. or Wy.	Dry fly
Catfish	Mississippi R.	Bologna sandwich
Shark	Okla. or Tex.	Oil Co.*

POLO AND HORSERACING

Horseracing, which offers big action and big depreciation-tax write offs is traditionally the Mogul's first choice, but polo, because it was originally played with the heads of political dissenters, has the inside track image-wise, and now leads by a head.

Polo kit:
1. $250,000 extra per year
2. Three Argentinians (if Mogul mounts)
   Four Argentinians (if Mogul only bets)
3. Ball
4. Mallet
5. String of ponies

SKIING

Ski at: Aspen, Vail, Sun Valley, with family.
    Also ski in Switzerland, when visiting Swiss bank account. Stay at your private chalet. To get to top of ski run: Take helicopter.

TEAM SPORT

Buy a team.

HINTS

Only Mini-Moguls bowl.

Only Yoguls arm-wrestle.

---

* *Moguls don't have time for quizzes. The listings are correctly matched.*

18

THE TIP OF THE ICEBERG

Grease is cheaper than steel.
—RUSTBELT WISDOM

*U*nlike the merely rich, Moguls always tip the deserving.

The Mogul Pocket Guide to Gratuities

STIMULUS	NAME OF GRATUITY	$ AMT.
Maître d' (for table)	"100 good reasons"	100
Convention hostess (for services rendered)	"a little present"	100
Current wife (for disregarding services rendered above)	"a little birthday present"	100,000 (in gems)
Top corporate execs	"stock option"	negotiable
Company spies	"business gift"	case Scotch
Industrial spies	"consultation fee"	negotiable
Shareholders	"dividends"	optional

Mayor (at his $500/plate fundraising dinner)	"a table"	5,000
In-laws, hangers-on	10 seats at mayoral fundraiser	0
Democratic Party	"contribution"	30,000
Republican Party	"dues"	130,000
Committee to reelect Republicans	"gambling loss"	70,000
Democratic Senator's favorite charity	"gift"	1,000
Republican Senator's old law firm	"retainer"	5,000
Armed citizens' group which says Republicans don't go far enough	"office equipment"	17,000
Police Benevolent Assn.	"token of appreciation"	1,000
Mogul Benevolent Assn. (Mogul tax lobby)	"membership"	50,000
Museum (so they will name a wing after you)	"immortality"	your art collection
Customs official	"misc. tips"	100
Caribbean provincial governor (or other foreign official in country with which you do business)	"misc. bus. exp."	230,000
N.Y. Times Magazine	"advertising"	1,300,000

*If the rich could hire people
to die for them, the poor could
make a wonderful living.*
—YIDDISH PROVERB

Endgame

Once you've achieved True Moguldom, you've got only two things to
worry about:
1. Losing your money
2. Losing your life
If you face these threats with courage
and cunning, neither need stop you.
In fact, death and ruin can both be
pluses in the long run because, taken
in tandem, they can augment your
mystique and thus increase your
chances for immortality.

19

WHEN MOGULS FALTER

*Going down with the ship is
the coward's way out.*

—CAPT. MOGUL IN "THE MOGUL STOOD
ON THE BURNING DECK"

*H*eadline: "Mogul Empire in Ruins!"—this is every Mogul's nightmare. Impossible as it seems when you're at the height of your powers, deep down you know that there are as many ways to lose your fortune as there are to increase it.

The fact is, most Mogul mishaps, as the Hunts (Bunker and Herbert), the Davises (Cullen and Ken), and (Big) John De Lorean will be quick to admit, are results of external factors and not of Mogul error.

MOGUL power failure is often due to:

Opening oil field in Libya
Opening auto factory in Ireland
Betting inflation will keep going up
Investing in South African *Krugerrand*
Illegally manipulating silver/drug prices
Getting caught
Refusing an offer you can't refuse
Using brother-in-law as lawyer
Spending too much time behind
    bars in Allenwood
Spending too much time holding
    up bar at "21"
Spending too much

The Mogul hears sad news of the business fortunes of a close Mogul friend

But regardless of who or what's to blame for Mogul woes, the True Mogul doesn't let catastrophe stop him/her. The True Mogul sees failure as an opportunity. An opportunity to:

Become a Legend in Your Lifetime

A meteoric rise and fall excites the public imagination. It's the stuff of myth. The stuff gods are made of. So don't hide your disgrace. Advertise it. Capitalize on it. Profit from it.

1 Pose, "proud in the face of adversity," with spouse for Avedon in *Vogue*. Pose alone, wearing a barrel, for Annie Leibovitz. Tell *People* what a relief it is not to be a slave to material things anymore. Tell *New York Magazine*, "Now I know how [Nixon, Carter, Napoleon, King Lear] felt." Make no secret of your visit to the Betty Ford Center.
2. Find God. Declare bankruptcy. Erase all debts.
3. Make comeback (instructions follow).

Your Comeback

Come out of jail and promote book.
Borrow from the little people.
Accept gifts.
Pawn gifts.
Invest money.

As Captain Mogul said, "Never let go unless you're in shallow water."

20

WHEN MOGULS FALL

*One should never worry
about money. Good health
and a few good friends are all
you need.*

—BUNKER HUNT, DOWN TO HIS LAST
FEW BILLION

*Dead gamblers don't have
any friends.* —SAM SPADE

*B*ecause illness endangers a Mogul's deal-making ability, a sick Mogul is a cranky Mogul.

The Good News

The good news is that state-of-the-art medical care can keep you fit and feisty in situations which cause others to draw up their wills.

Moguls don't get black lung, sickle-cell anemia, or scurvy. Moguls don't get wounded in knife fights.

Sick Moguls don't "go to the doctor"; they "fly in my man." "My man" is the chief resident specialist at the best hospital in the world in whatever's bothering the Mogul.

Very sick Moguls don't "go to the hospital," they "check into my wing"—the one they donated to the local hospital. (Donating the whole hospital is even better.)

Moguls don't go into nursing homes, they have private nurses who look good in bathing suits.

Terminally ill Moguls don't always die. Moguls get first pick of human and artificial parts when theirs malfunction, and Moguls can afford treatments whose expense would kill the average person.

SPARE PARTS
HEART $ ...
LIVER $ ...
KIDNEYS $ ...
BRAIN $ ...
LEFT EYE $ ...
KNEECAP $ ...
SHIN $ ...
PELVIS $ ...

Moguls don't "send
for the priest"
because they have private
chapels, and anyway . . .

Moguls don't repent.

The Bad News

The bad news is that an excess of success *can* be lethal. Barbara Hutton and Howard Hughes proved conclusively that

You CAN be too rich and too thin!

Moguls are prey to skin diseases from having
Too much sun
Too much gold in jewelry (anything over 18 karats can cause skin
   irritations)
Perfume that's too expensive (Berloque dermatitis leaves a green
   rash around the neck)
A vacation that's too tropical (mango dermatitis from mango skin
   and physophoto-dermatitis as a result of mixing margaritas with
   Acapulco sun)

Moguls are also prone to deafness (selective) and bad eyesight—from squinting at fine print on contracts, gazing off at their farthest oil well, or staring underlings down. Rather than worry about glasses, have your windows and windshields ground to your prescription.

The Really Bad News

The really bad news is that Moguls do die. The important thing to remember in this regard is: it is better to be dead than to be declared mentally incompetent.

Make sure you have a cyanide pill in each house, plane, and boat.

When you feel you must die, be sure to . . .

DIE A MOGUL'S DEATH.

Die either: (a) laughing all the way to the bank, or (b) while "giving dictation" to your secretary at ten p.m. in an apartment no one knew you had. (You'll be remembered longer.)

DON'T DIE:

In the middle of a divorce
Wearing black leather (except for your boots)
Wearing frilly underwear (Mogulines excepted)
With food in your mouth (muffles your last words)

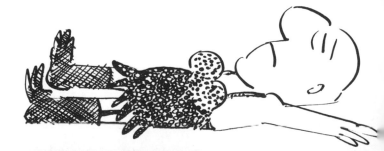

And whatever you do, don't despair, because, for Moguls there can be . . .

21

LIFE AFTER DEATH

Curtain! Fast music! Lights!
Ready for the last finale!
Great! The show looks good.
The show looks good.

—LAST WORDS OF FLORENZ ZIEGFELD
(1867–1932)

*M*ost people only live once, but why should you be one of them? It is every Mogul's dream to achieve immortality, and there are only two ways to do it.

1. Earn it.
2. Buy it.

Of these, the second is the most dependable. To be a legend in your own time takes money, but to be a legend in someone else's takes more money.

There are nine methods for buying immortality now on the market. They are: Wings, Words, Wills, Stones, Sperm, Space, Film, Freezing, and Folly.

Method 1: Wings

A Mogul, like an angel, needs wings. Only, your wings are named after you. Hospital, museum, and university library wings are the most popular with Moguls, though some, like Dorothy Chandler of Los Angeles, prefer the word "pavilion."

Method 2: Words

When near death write a memoir betraying many people's intimate confidences and portraying self as hero(ine). Finance mini-series on self. Also, try to utter famous last words like Adam Smith's oft-repeated "I believe we must adjourn this meeting to some other place."

Method 3: Wills

Write a will so contestable that family lawsuits will keep you in the press for generations. Howard Hughes' artistry with a will surpassed even Pablo Picasso's.

Alternatively, establish a foundation or annual prize. A good Mogul foundation is one which uses your money to disassociate you from everything which made you rich.

IF YOU MADE YOUR FORTUNE IN	FUND
Pumping crude	Art
Strip mining	The Sierra Club

IF YOU INVENTED	LEAVE YOUR MONEY TO
Mass production	Birth control
Dynamite	A peace prize

119

Method 4: Sperm

The field of sperm banking is wide open to anyone with a couple of afternoons free for stocking the bank's coffers. For female Moguls and squeamish males, cloning is a better bet. Set up a foundation to preserve some of your cells with their DNA intact, so thousands of genetic replicas of you can be hatched once science knows how.

Method 5: Space

At $10,000 per pound, burial in space is one of the best plans now available for Moguls. Space, free of relatives, foreigners, and bacteria is the one place you can be sure you'll last forever. Because of the expense, many rich people send only their ashes; but this precludes cloning, so, Moguls, resist the temptation to cut corners.

Three orbits are being offered, two circling the earth and one straight out into Nowhere. Nowhere is the one you want. It's tempting to think of your kids watching you through their telescopes as you orbit through the night sky, but one "Star Wars" attack by the Russians and you could lose your entire investment, so you're better off taking the chance of being found in bullrushes on another planet and cloned by aliens.

Method 6: Stones

Build a monument or mausoleum exaggerating your importance and achievements. The Pharaoh Ramses II, after losing to the Hittites, built a memorial to his fictitious victory which won him over three thousand years of good publicity.

If you don't want to build a pyramid, try to get buried in Arlington, Westminster Abbey, or anyplace tombs get noticed.

Method 7: Film

It is rumored that near the end, Walt Disney prefilmed instructions to management to be viewed in annual installments after his death. This method of creating an "afterlife" for yourself is almost as good as being reborn as Michael Eisner.

Method 8: Freezing

Occasionally Moguls request in their wills that they be fast-frozen and their bodies kept at subzero temperatures in case someone finds:

    a. A cure for what killed them, and . . .

    b. A way to bring back the dead

BREAK ICE
IN 2100 A.D.

This technique, known as cryogenics, is a long shot, but Moguls are risk-takers. If you go this route, make sure your tomb has an auxiliary generator on automatic backup in case of brown-outs.

Method 9: Folly

The final proof of immortality is when a crazy person imagines he's you. You can't force lunatics to choose you as their delusion of grandeur, but the smart Mogul creates an identity competitive with that of Napoleon, the Marquis de Sade and Joan of Arc, and so increases his edge in the nutcake market once in a Better World.

22

LIFE AFTER THE APOCALYPSE

Après moi, who cares?

—LOUIS XIV, THE SUN MOGUL

*M*ogul spaceships are secretly under
construction on Mogul launch pads all over the
world! Trial flights of Mogul spacecraft
(mistaken for U.F.O.s by the naive) have
been going on since the forties!
Sound crazy? Maybe it does—now. But
remember: when the going gets tough, the
tough dismantle everything and sell it off for
real estate. Because no one is sure the world
won't blow up tomorrow, and since saving the
Earth isn't cost effective, more and more
Moguls are looking to Outer Space as the best
place to establish an Immortal Name.

All Moguls plan an exodus if there's an apocalypse,
of course, but many can't wait that long for lift-off. The minute
science invents a pinstripe space suit, Mogul pioneers will head for
greener galaxies. After all, Outer Space is ideal Mogul territory: no taxes,
no regulatory agencies, no consumer groups, no terrorist kidnappers or unions.
Outer Space, in short, is pure opportunity. *It's rich in minerals! Challenge!*
Adventure! And best of all, it's Big! So, see you there.

The Armchair Mogul Quiz

Circle the answer in each group that does NOT belong.

EXAMPLE:

Mogul fantasies are:
a. Doing it all over again
b. Doing it twice in one night
c. Waking up tall
d. Doing drugs with the Stones

Moguls are instantly recognizable by:
a. Their lack of coats, hats, and umbrellas
b. Their jets
c. Six A.M.
d. Their gentle eyes

Moguls don't ever:
a. Wait in line
b. Wait table
c. Wait
d. Wait until a stock goes down, then buy lots of it

Moguls say:
a. "If I don't get it some other Mogul will."
b. "If it is worth fighting for, it is worth fighting dirty for."
c. "If you think I got where I am by polishing pulpits, you're a damn fool."
d. "Have a nice day."

Falling Moguls say:
a. "Cocaine? I thought you were selling *propane*!"
b. "There are germs on my food."

c. "Any man who knows exactly how much money he is worth isn't worth very much."

d. "By the time my guys get through with the numbers, we know those [target] companies better than they know themselves."

A Mystery Mogul would do anything for his:
a. Mother
b. Mob
c. Polo pony
d. Mate

An Upwardly Mogul wouldn't be caught dead in:
a. Silk kimonos
b. Shamrocks
c. Fringed buckskin chaps like Cornelia Guest's
d. Schmatas (trans. "rags")

Moguls listen to:
a. Nobody
b. Frank Sinatra
c. The news
d. Guests

A Mogul's ideal dinner guest might be:
a. Dr. No
b. Mr. T.
c. Mr. Ed
d. O

Moguls call:
a. Prenuptial agreements "prenupes"
b. Money "money"
c. Spades "spades"
d. Wives "my dearest darling, light of my life"

For a Megalomogul, doing deals comes as naturally as:
a. Breathing
b. Being in love (with self)
c. Winning
d. Birthin' babies

Moguls secretly fear:
a. Nader's raiders
b. The deficit
c. Waking up shorter
d. National indifference toward the poor

ANSWERS: The last answer never belongs.